100
BIBLE PRAYERS
FOR MEN

ELIJAH ADKINS

100
BIBLE PRAYERS
FOR MEN

Devotions and Direction
on Talking with God

BARBOUR
PUBLISHING

© 2024 by Barbour Publishing, Inc.

ISBN 978-1-63609-809-8

All rights reserved. No part of this publication may be reproduced or transmitted for commercial purposes, except for brief quotations in printed reviews, without written permission of the publisher. Reproduced text may not be used on the World Wide Web.

Churches and other noncommercial interests may reproduce portions of this book without the express written permission of Barbour Publishing, provided that the text does not exceed 500 words and that the text is not material quoted from another publisher. When reproducing text from this book, include the following credit line: "From 100 *Bible Prayers for Men*, published by Barbour Publishing, Inc. Used by permission."

All scripture quotations are taken from the Barbour Simplified KJV, copyright © 2022 by Barbour Publishing, Inc., Uhrichsville, Ohio 44683. All rights reserved.

Cover Design: Greg Jackson, Thinkpen Design

Published by Barbour Publishing, Inc., 1810 Barbour Drive, Uhrichsville, Ohio 44683, www.barbourbooks.com

Our mission is to inspire the world with the life-changing message of the Bible.

ecpa Member of the
Evangelical Christian
Publishers Association

Printed in China.

The Bible is packed with prayers, and they all offer guidance to us today.

From Genesis to Revelation, prayer is defined, described, and demanded. At its most basic level, prayer is simply talking with God—what could possibly be more important and fulfilling?

This book highlights many powerful prayers from scripture, making them the basis of practical and encouraging devotions. You'll learn the meaning and purpose of each prayer along with ways to apply it to your own life.

In the pages that follow, you'll dig deeper into biblical accounts of prayer, such as Nehemiah's quick, silent request while talking with King Artaxerxes; Daniel's confession of his nation's sins; the servant of Abraham's prayer for success in his duties; Peter's "Save me!" as he plunged into the Sea of Galilee; and Jesus' model prayer spoken in response to the disciple's request, "Teach us to pray."

The one hundred entries are grouped into eight overarching themes:

Communicating with God is vital for healthy spiritual living. Find the insights you need in *100 Bible Prayers for Men*.

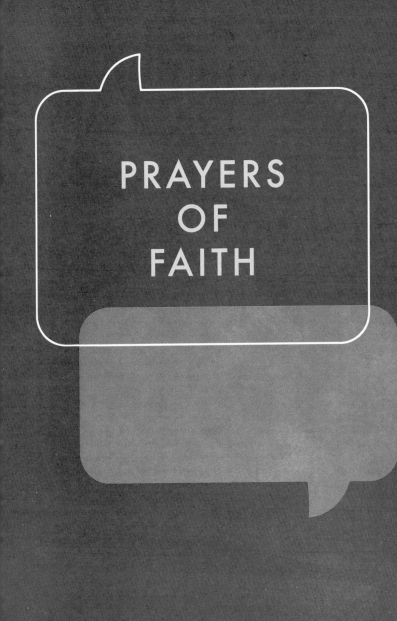

PRAYERS
OF
FAITH

THE FAITH PARADOX

"Lord, I believe; help my unbelief."
MARK 9:24

One day, a man came to Jesus with an unusual request: he wanted the Lord to heal his demon-possessed son. For years, this child had suffered in the grip of a dark presence, turning each day into a living nightmare. So when the father heard of Jesus—a mysterious miracleman who was passing by that day—he chose to believe his son would be healed.

Today's verse poignantly illustrates the paradox of faith. When we choose to believe in God—to throw ourselves headlong into a commitment to a Creator we've never seen—an ocean of uncertainty stands in our way. For a brief period, faith and doubt blend into a single, heartfelt cry, "I believe; help my unbelief."

On our own, such a commitment would be impossible. Humans are wired to accept only what we see and understand. But God, recognizing our limitations, reaches down and pierces the veil separating us from the divine, beckoning us to take His hand. It's at this intersection—where the physical meets the spiritual—that faith triumphs over unbelief.

Do you ever feel like the man in today's verse? Do you have a passion for serving God. . .but feel weighted down by troubling questions? If so, don't try to hide it from Him; He already knows. Instead, keep reaching for God's hand, searching for Him with all your heart, and it's guaranteed that—in the moment You least expect it—He will break through with a miracle.

FOR FURTHER THOUGHT:

- Why do you think God lets us doubt sometimes?

- When has your faith been the weakest?

- How did that story end?

PRAYER STARTER:

Father, my faith is sometimes riddled with doubts. Through Your Holy Spirit, teach me how to lean on Your invisible promises.

THE "HOUND OF HEAVEN"

"My Lord and my God."
JOHN 20:28

The nineteenth-century poet Francis Thompson wrote a piece titled, "The Hound of Heaven." It describes a man fleeing God's presence, unwilling to be found or loved by his Creator. But God never stops pursuing, and the narrator eventually gives in under the weight of God's mercy and grace.

The apostle Thomas was a bit like the narrator in that poem. Shaken and hollowed out by Jesus' crucifixion, Thomas had determined in his heart never to allow himself to hope for a miracle again. So when Jesus' disciples announced the astounding news that Jesus was alive, Thomas scoffed. "Unless I see in His hands the print of the nails, and put my finger into the print of the nails, and thrust my hand into His side," he stubbornly proclaimed, "I will not believe" (John 20:25).

Jesus could have shunned Thomas in response. He could have given His disciple a self-fulfilling prophecy, hiding from Thomas' doubting eyes. But instead, Jesus appeared to Thomas in dramatic fashion, giving him just what he needed for belief. At this point, Thomas had a choice: Would he shut his eyes to the truth or give in to the love standing before him?

Thankfully, he chose the latter.

Do you sometimes find yourself running from God's promises? Have you been so hurt and disillusioned that you find it hard to trust again? If so, God isn't giving up on you. He's standing before you today, reaching out His hand with an offer of unlimited love and blessings.

Are you ready to give in?

FOR FURTHER THOUGHT:

- How has your faith been shaken in the past?
- How did Jesus reveal Himself in that situation to strengthen your faith?
- What are some other ways God offers proof of His existence and mercy today?

PRAYER STARTER:

Father, I'm through with running. My eyes have searched for far too long. The truth is right in front of me. I surrender.

MORE THAN A CLICHÉ

"Lord, to whom shall we go? You have the words of eternal life. And we believe and are sure that You are the Christ, the Son of the living God."

JOHN 6:68–69

Peter, despite his limited and flawed knowledge of God's ultimate plan at the time, understood something that everyone else in his day had missed: Jesus Christ is the answer.

"Yeah, yeah," you may say, "I've seen and heard that a thousand times. It's plastered on everything from church signs to bumper stickers." And sure, you may know it's true and receive constant reminders of it throughout your day, but do you *live* like it's true? Are you just dipping your toes in the water of faith, going through the motions and saying all the right words? Or have you, like Peter, taken the plunge? Have you willingly abandoned your old way of life, recognizing its ultimate futility, and leaped headlong into God's plan?

Jesus is not a "fill-in-the-blank" answer. Life is more than a game of Bible trivia; it's a perpetual war against the forces of meaninglessness and despair. And in that sense, Jesus is the answer—your one and only battle plan, your ammunition against hell itself. When it comes to the war of faith, nice platitudes and bumper-sticker theology just won't cut it. It takes a gritty determination to follow Jesus.

Do you have that kind of faith today?

FOR FURTHER THOUGHT:

- What do you need to forsake as you surrender to the Lord?

- Why do you think God won't accept half-hearted devotion?

PRAYER STARTER:

Lord Jesus, I believe in You. And this doesn't just mean I simply understand You exist—it means I'm committed to following You as my one and only solution.

WAR OF THE WORLDVIEWS

"Hear me, O Lord, hear me, that this people may know that You are the Lord God and that You have turned their hearts back again."
1 Kings 18:37

The prophet Elijah must have had a lot of confidence in God. To ask God for a miracle is one thing, but to do it in front of hundreds of pagan priests in a challenge that would decisively prove who's really in charge? *That* takes faith.

After preparing a stone altar, laying a bull on top, and drenching it with as much water as he could find, Elijah called on God to send down a fire so hot that it would not only ignite the sacrifice but turn the altar itself to cinders. You can imagine the stunned look on his audience's faces as Elijah's mighty prayer poured from his lips. Then, as the final words of his plea hung in the dry, dusty air, a bolt from the blue blinded the crowd, followed by a deafening crack of thunder. As the white-hot fire engulfed the altar, one fact became apparent—the true God had spoken, and His name wasn't Baal.

Today, Christian men find themselves in a "war

of the worldviews." As culture becomes increasingly hostile toward God and His righteousness, the need for men of God to step up becomes greater each day. It's time for us to pray with the fervent faith of Elijah, asking God to send His fire and consume all hearts with His love.

The outcome is settled: God has already won the war. Are you willing to fight?

FOR FURTHER THOUGHT:

- How can you be so close to God that you believe He'll answer outrageous prayers?
- What "crazy prayer" would you like to pray to God?

PRAYER STARTER:

God, show Yourself to this world. Send a revival, spurred on by Your unstoppable Spirit, that all might see Your glory.

TOO LATE

"My daughter is even now dead, but come and lay Your hand on her and she shall live."

MATTHEW 9:18

The ruler's story was over. He could do nothing. His daughter lay dead at home. The time for miracles was past. All he could do was accept his loss with cruel tears.

Except. . .he still had faith.

This man, whom the Gospel of Luke identifies as Jairus (8:41), knew that the power Jesus possessed hadn't been seen in Israel for hundreds of years—maybe never. If anyone could bring his daughter back from the dead, Jesus was the man for the job. Even in the face of hopelessness—even after his daughter had breathed her last—Jairus ran to Jesus with one urgent request: "Lay Your hand on her and she shall live."

How many Christian men today have Jairus' faith? When the forces of darkness are towering over us, laughing and claiming victory, what's our response? To just put our heads down and give in? Or to look up to heaven, hoping for one last miracle?

Whether it's an unsaved friend or family member who seems too far gone to accept the gospel, a financial disaster that threatens to take your livelihood or even your home, or a doctor's report with a disturbing sense of finality, no situation is ever so hopeless that God can't handle it. As Jairus' prayer—and Jesus' corresponding miracle—proves, "too late" is when God does His strongest work.

FOR FURTHER THOUGHT:

- When have you seen God turn a situation around, even after it seemed too late?
- How did that affect your faith?

PRAYER STARTER:

I'm not giving up or giving in, Lord. I'll keep praying for Your will to be done, even after all hope seems lost.

OPEN MINDED

"Lord, I believe."
JOHN 9:38

The blind man who spoke today's prayer was the epitome of an open-minded person. After obeying Jesus' instructions by washing in the pool of Siloam, the man was faced with the shocking truth: he could see again. For the first time in his life, colors and shapes flashed in his field of vision, overwhelming him with a sense of liberation and unbridled joy.

The religious leaders, however, were a little less enthusiastic. They found the man and immediately began grilling him about Jesus' identity. "Who was this guy?" they asked him repeatedly, trying to pressure him into admitting Jesus was a sinner. But the man, knowing something amazing had happened and unable to mask the truth, wasn't willing to play their games. "If this man were not of God," he eventually retorted, "He could do nothing" (John 9:33). His faith was incomplete at this stage, yet he was exactly where Jesus wanted him—at the doorstep of truth, eager for God to let him in.

And that's what Jesus did. When He came to the man later and revealed his identity as the Messiah, the formerly blind man could do nothing but say, "Lord, I believe." It was that simple. No grappling with the truth, no trying to bend it to his own favor, no attempt to rationalize away the obvious. Just an honest, sincere expression of faith—a faith rooted in his undeniable encounter with the divine.

When God reveals Himself to you by speaking to your heart or through the pages of His Word, are you like this blind man, eager to accept what He says?

FOR FURTHER THOUGHT:

- What is your default response when God reveals Himself to you?
- Why did the religious leaders miss the truth while a "commoner" understood it perfectly?

PRAYER STARTER:

Lord, because I know You are holy and cannot lie, I believe every promise You make. I place my trust in You as the only source of perfect truth.

And he stretched himself over the child three times, and cried to the LORD, and said, "O LORD my God, I ask you, let this child's soul come into him again."
1 KINGS 17:21

Today's prayer is unique for two reasons: (1) its bold nature, and (2) the strange actions Elijah performed while praying.

What was the point of Elijah stretching himself over the child's body three times? Was this some sort of magic ritual? Or was Elijah merely following instructions from God, who enabled him to perform such miracles? Obviously, Elijah wasn't a magician; he was a prophet. So the second scenario has to be true. But that begs another question: Why on earth would God do it like *that*?

Nobody knows the answer to this question. . .and we probably never will. But Elijah didn't have to know the answer—as long as God said it, that settled it. No need for further questions.

The church would be so effective if men of God had Elijah's faith. Instead of waffling every time God tells them to do something that seems a bit strange, they'd jump headlong into the assignment, no questions asked. One act of obedience at a time, Christian men would start changing the world through their prayers of faith.

Does this sound like a world you'd love to live in? If so, what are you waiting for? Start making the change today.

FOR FURTHER THOUGHT:

- When has God told you to do something that seemed nonsensical?
- How did you respond?
- What was the outcome?

PRAYER STARTER:

Father God, I'm willing to obey You today, no matter how odd Your instructions might seem. Grant me the faith to step out of my comfort zone and start changing the world for You.

EYES OF FAITH

"LORD, it is nothing for You to help, whether with many or with those who have no power."

2 CHRONICLES 14:11

With this prayer, King Asa made a molehill out of a mountain.

Facing down an army of one million men and three hundred chariots (2 Chronicles 14:9), Asa had every reason to be afraid. This number was nearly twice the size of Israel's army. Even if Israel managed to hold their own, the best they could hope for would be a stalemate. . .but only after a bloodbath of literally biblical proportions.

But Asa had one thing that his enemy did not: God's support. So Asa, knowing his nation's history and having learned all the right lessons from it, wasn't afraid. "LORD," he prayed, "it is nothing for You to help." That's right—compared to God's power, an army of one million is *nothing*. God had given Asa eyes of faith, and Asa carried this divinely granted vision triumphantly into battle, trouncing his enemies so thoroughly that they surrendered in exhaustion and fear (14:13–14).

Imagine having the faith of King Asa. Imagine waking

up each morning surrounded by the dark forces of the world and saying, "God, all that is nothing to me as long as You're by my side." Well, you don't have to imagine it because that's the kind of power God grants His children. Each day, He's offering you the chance to see the world through eyes of faith. Are you willing to accept?

FOR FURTHER THOUGHT:

- What "army" are you facing—a financial situation, physical challenges, mockery for your faith, or something else?
- How can you better trust God to fight for you?

PRAYER STARTER:

All-powerful God, You're awesome in might— far beyond my ability to comprehend. Nothing— not even the battle up ahead—is too hard for You.

OFF-ROAD SOLUTIONS

"Lord, I am not worthy that You should come under my roof. But only speak the word, and my servant shall be healed."

MATTHEW 8:8

Today's prayer was spoken by a centurion with desperate faith. His servant had fallen gravely ill, to the point that he was "paralyzed" and "grievously tormented" (Matthew 8:6). By all appearances, death knocked at his door.

So what did the centurion ask Jesus to do? To rush to his house and lay His hands on the suffering man? Well, that's what most people would have asked. . .but not this Roman soldier. Instead, he said, "Only speak the word, and my servant shall be healed." This man had such a deep understanding of Jesus' power that he knew His physical presence wasn't even required for the miracle to take place—all that was needed was Jesus' word.

How often do we Christian men try putting God in a box in our prayers? "I want You to do this," we say, and then we give Him instructions about how we want it done. We plot out God's plans *for* Him, using a neat, tidy roadmap that we can easily understand. But as the centurion understood, God loves tearing up our maps and off-roading through the wilderness. His methods are often unorthodox, and it takes a spiritually open-minded man to see an opportunity where none seems available.

Embrace God's offroad solutions. It's a fascinating journey.

FOR FURTHER THOUGHT:

- How often do your expectations of the way you think God will work come true?
- How can you start broadening your understanding of His power today?

PRAYER STARTER:

Lord, I know You can do anything, even things that most would call impossible. I'm willing to let You work in my life in unexpected ways.

SUPREME CONFIDENCE

"For I know that my Redeemer lives and that He shall stand at the latter day on the earth. And though after my skin worms destroy this body, yet in my flesh I shall see God."
JOB 19:25–26

Some scholars believe that Job was the first book of the Bible written. Whether that's true, we'll probably never know. What we do know is that Job lived long, long before Jesus' birth. . .and perhaps even before the law of Moses. Yet in today's passage, we see that Job somehow had a strong understanding of God's character.

"I know that my Redeemer lives," Job cried out in the midst of pain. Even as the monstrous forms of disease, death, and suffering loomed over his frail, shaking body, Job remembered how closely he had walked with his Maker all those years. He didn't understand why he suffered or even if he would escape death, but his heart rested on one rock-solid truth: God is alive. And as long as God lives, there is hope: "And though after my skin worms destroy this body, yet in my flesh I shall see God."

Job knew—despite the complete lack of concrete evidence—that injustice would never have the final say. Even though his understanding of the afterlife was incomplete, he knew—based entirely on God's character—that death would never be the end.

Are you supremely confident that your Redeemer lives? If so, proclaim it today. Declare to God your certainty in His promises.

FOR FURTHER THOUGHT:

- When you are suffering, how can you exhibit hope in your Redeemer?
- How do we as Christians have even greater access to faith than Job did?

PRAYER STARTER:

Holy God, I don't know much about this life, and I certainly don't know much about the life to come. But I do know this: You're alive, and one day I will see you face to face. I can't wait for that day!

IMPULSIVE FAITH

And Peter answered Him and said, "Lord, if it is You, bid me to come to You on the water."
MATTHEW 14:28

The Bible contains many examples of ordinary men displaying extraordinary faith—David, Gideon, Noah, Abraham, Paul, Elijah. . .and the list goes on. But today's prayer might just be the purest, most exemplary instance of faith in God's Word.

Peter, prior to his encounter with Jesus, was nothing more than a lowly fisherman with a temper. He acted on impulse, jumping into fights and arguments with scarcely a thought of the consequences. But on this day, God would begin redeeming Peter's rash, impulsive behavior. How? By focusing his confidence on Jesus, not Peter's own abilities.

Many think of impulsiveness as a fault—and to some degree, it is. But when this impulsiveness is directed toward your obedience to God, it takes the form of childlike faith (Matthew 18:3). Obedient kids don't care if their parents' instructions seem strange—they just obey instinctively, unconcerned about the "what ifs." Similarly, Peter didn't care if walking on water was normally impossible—all he cared about was getting to Jesus. If he had to break a few laws of nature to do so, then so be it. God was able.

Maybe you struggle with impulsive behavior. Maybe you've begged God to change your personality. . .when all along, what you should be asking is for God to use your personality to advance His kingdom, shifting your confidence from yourself toward God. Maybe then you can pray with Peter, "Lord, if it is You, bid me to come to You on the water."

FOR FURTHER THOUGHT:

- How did God use Peter's impulsiveness later in his life?

- What other typically negative character traits can God redeem for His purposes?

PRAYER STARTER:

I don't care if it's impossible, God—I'm willing to follow where You lead, even if it means stepping on the waves.

GOING ALL THE WAY

"Master, I will follow You wherever You go."
MATTHEW 8:19

On the surface, today's prayer sounded simple enough. As Jesus taught the multitudes, walked along the shoreline of the Sea of Galilee, and crossed various territories, it must have been exciting for new converts to jump on board this journey of learning God's truth. A little walking, a lot of listening, and a liberation from one's old, dusty routines sounded like an offer too good to pass up—hence the crowds.

But this illusion of an easy-going life didn't last long. Looking at today's prayer, it's easy to forget that Jesus' travels finally brought Him to a place that nobody wanted to go: to the cross.

Suddenly, the innumerable crowds dwindled to a devoted few. . .and even most of these close followers deserted Him as the danger became too great. We don't know if the man who prayed today's verse stuck by Jesus' side through it all, but it's safe to say he did not have a painful crucifixion in mind when he said these words.

But in order to live the Christian life, the cross is a must. It may not be a literal plank of wood with nails, but it *will* involve suffering and heartbreak. Following in Jesus' footsteps means stepping with Him into places we would otherwise avoid. It's not an easy path, but as Jesus' resurrection would eventually prove, it will be well worth it in the end.

FOR FURTHER THOUGHT:

- In what ways are you dying to yourself today as you follow Christ?

- How far would you follow Jesus down a path you never intended to travel on?

PRAYER STARTER:

Father, I'll admit—the thought of taking up my cross isn't too thrilling. . .but if that's what it takes to follow You, then I'm all in.

PRAYERS
FOR
FORGIVENESS

HEAD TO TOE

"Lord, [wash] not only my feet,
but also my hands and my head."
JOHN 13:9

When Jesus announced his plans to wash Peter's feet, Peter had some thoughts. "You shall never wash my feet" (John 13:8) he exclaimed, no doubt wondering why the Son of God would even think about performing such a menial task for a sinful man like him. But Jesus responded, "If I do not wash you, you have no part with Me" (13:8). Suddenly, Peter changed his tone completely. "Lord," he cried impulsively, "not only my feet, but also my hands and my head."

Looking back, it's clear that the act of washing Peter's feet symbolized Jesus' forgiveness—without which we cannot enter the kingdom of God. But even with the benefit of hindsight, how often do we act like Peter, balking at the idea that God could descend to our level and wash us of our filthiness? We may refuse to ask for forgiveness, assuming that to do so would be the height of disrespect. *I'm too far gone*, we tell ourselves. *God would never waste His time on a sinner like me.*

But the good news is that Jesus' forgiveness has no

limits. It's free for anyone who comes to Him—from the rich philanthropist who's made a name for himself in the world of charity foundations, to the poor, drug-addled child molester in the back alley, ready to take his life. All are free to come to Him. . .and all will find His arms opened wide in love.

Today, don't be afraid to ask Jesus to wash you— head to toe.

FOR FURTHER THOUGHT:

- In what ways do you act like Peter when God wants to stoop to your level to clean you?
- How can Jesus' example of washing Peter's feet spur you on to serve and forgive your brothers and sisters in Christ when they sin against you?

PRAYER STARTER:

Lord Jesus, wash me clean of my past misdeeds. I know I'm not worthy, but I'm asking for a thorough cleansing today.

WASHED AWAY

*Have mercy on me, O God, according to
Your loving-kindness; according to the
multitude of Your tender mercies, blot out my
transgressions. Wash me thoroughly from
my iniquity, and cleanse me from my sin.*
PSALM 51:1–2

We all know the story of David and Bathsheba—the
time when the "man after [God's] own heart" (1 Samuel
13:14) had a man killed in order to steal his wife. This
shocking story proves that nobody—not even the best
of us—is immune to sin's allure.

David had not only fallen into the mud pit—he'd
leaped giddily, cannonball style, as if trying to make the
biggest splash he could. But even though his sin was
ugly, his prayer in today's verse is unmistakably beauti-
ful. "Have mercy on me," he cried to God, knowing there
wasn't a reason in the world that would compel God to
do so. . .except that God's love knows no bounds. "Wash
me," he prayed, disgusted by the stench of the misdeeds
that clung to his soul. "Cleanse me from my sin."

We all have a "David and Bathsheba" moment—a sin
that defines our primary faults and forever stains our

memories. Some are more minor than others, but the guilt can feel crushing all the same. But there's good news: even the worst crime against God's holiness can be washed away as if it never happened. If we are truly sorry, we can speak today's prayer to God, knowing He will be more than willing to cleanse us from our iniquities.

FOR FURTHER THOUGHT:

- When have you felt beyond God's reach—as if your past sins are too numerous to be forgiven?

- What would have happened to Israel if David had thought this?

PRAYER STARTER:

I'm sorry, Lord. I know I don't deserve Your mercy, but I also know You promise to give it whenever I ask. So that's what I'm asking for today.

REGRET

And he said to Jesus, "Lord, remember me
when You come into Your kingdom."
LUKE 23:42

As the thief hung on the cross, there was only one
thing more painful than the spikes in his wrists and
the lung-crushing weight of his own body stretched out
on a cruel plank of wood: his memories. Like a broken
faucet, the memories of the crimes that led him to this
excruciating moment drowned his mind with regret.
His sins were many, and he was finally receiving his
just reward—right here, all at once.

But that's when he noticed Jesus beside him. What
was the supposed Son of God doing on a cross, dying
a criminal's death? At first, he scoffed at this suffering
Man. Surely, He'd been a fraud. Surely, God would never
allow His own Son to die like this. But then, maybe it
was the look in Jesus' eyes—that compassionate gaze
that He directed toward His tormentors. Maybe it was
Jesus' silence in the face of such pain. Or maybe it
was something far more mysterious—a hidden work of
God deep within his heart. Whatever it was, the thief
recognized two things: (1) This *was* the Son of God, and

(2) now was his only chance for redemption.

So even as mockery poured from the lips of everyone else, the dying thief uttered a simple plea for mercy to the only one who could grant it.

And mercy is exactly what Jesus gave him.

FOR FURTHER THOUGHT:

- What's the worst sin a person can commit?
- How can knowing that God will forgive even that sin compel you to ask Him to forgive your own?

PRAYER STARTER:

Lord God, I'm not proud of some of the things I've done. I know I deserve to be punished. . .but I'm asking for Your grace today. Please remember me in Your kingdom.

A BAD WAY TO PRAY

"The Pharisee stood by himself and prayed this: 'God, I thank You that I am not as other men are—extortioners, unjust, adulterers, or even as this tax collector.' . . . And the tax collector, standing afar off, would not so much as lift up his eyes to heaven, but struck his breast, saying, 'God, be merciful to me, a sinner.' "

LUKE 18:11, 13

If this book had a category named "Prayers *Not* to Pray," this Pharisee's prayer would probably be number one. Not only did this self-righteous religious leader commit the sins of bragging and speaking evil of others, but he also did it all under the guise of thanking God. Nothing enrages God more than when we try to smuggle pride in a box marked HOLINESS.

The tax collector, however, had the right idea. Instead of relying on his own efforts and snubbing his nose at anyone who didn't quite meet his standards, he realized an important truth: on his own, he had nothing. What possible motive would God have for offering the greatest gift in the universe to a scheming traitor who regularly cheated his own people? None. Yet the tax collector, crushed by the weight of a life poorly spent, still asked. . .and God answered (Luke 18:14).

When you mess up and kneel before God for mercy, don't begin by saying, "God, You know I'm not as bad as so-and-so next door." Instead, come to Him with the tax collector's attitude—a broken and contrite spirit (Psalm 51:17), humbly asking for His forgiveness.

FOR FURTHER THOUGHT:

- How have you been tempted to make excuses for yourself, even while asking for forgiveness?

- How might you gain an attitude of greater humility?

PRAYER STARTER:

Lord, I don't care about being better or worse than someone else. I want only to please You. Forgive me for all the times I've failed, and grant me grace to keep improving.

HUMBLE REPENTANCE

And it came to pass when Ahab heard those words, that he tore his clothes and put sackcloth on his body and fasted. . . . And the word of the LORD came to Elijah the Tishbite, saying, "See how Ahab humbles himself before Me? Because He humbles himself before Me, I will not bring the evil in his days."

1 KINGS 21:27–29

Out of all the evil kings in Israel's history, Ahab was near the top of the list. He openly disregarded God's commands, encouraged idol worship in the land, consented to an innocent man's death over a vineyard, and repeatedly expressed his hatred toward Elijah, God's prophet.

So imagine Elijah's surprise when Ahab repented. After receiving a particularly grim warning from God, Ahab finally came to his senses. Sackcloth and torn garments were universal signs of grief at the time, and fasting was a great way to show God how serious you were about something. So by doing all three, Ahab was humbly telling God, "You were right; I was wrong. Please forgive me." And God did. Even though there would still be consequences for Ahab's bad behavior, the terrible things God had promised would not befall him as long as he continued in his repentance.

If you've ever committed a sin so huge that you think it's impossible to find God's mercy, think again. Because of Jesus' death on the cross, God's grace literally knows no bounds. His mercy and love are free of charge. The only requirement is true repentance.

FOR FURTHER THOUGHT:

- Why do you think God requires an attitude of humility when we confess?
- Why doesn't the Lord wipe away all the consequences of our sin after He forgives us?

PRAYER STARTER:

Lord God, I know there's no way I can earn Your mercy, but I'm humbly asking for it nonetheless. Please extend Your grace to me today.

NO CONDEMNATION

*O Lord, do not rebuke me in Your wrath
or chasten me in Your hot displeasure.*

PSALM 38:1

Nobody wants to be judged by God. Because God is perfectly righteous—and because we are most certainly *not*—the unrepentant sinner has no hope of receiving His pardon. There's nothing in our lives, not even our greatest deed, that would merit an ounce of God's grace. All we deserve is His fiery, terrifying judgment.

Even David, who lived centuries before Jesus' birth, understood this horrifying truth. He knew that without God's grace, he was doomed. . .so all that was left for him to do was fall to his knees before the God who could judge him at a moment's notice. Like a misbehaving child before his parents, David pled for grace.

As Christians, we understand that Jesus' sacrifice was what made God's answer to David possible. Its effects reached back into time, covering the sins of God's people whenever they brought their humble, broken hearts before His feet. David didn't have the benefit of knowing where this mercy originated. . .but we do. We know that because God loves us so much,

45

He gave up His Son to prevent us from experiencing the terror of His wrath. Instead of relying on our own flawed natures, we can rely on Jesus' perfection to save us from certain doom.

Even when we deserve to die, we are free to ask God for life everlasting.

FOR FURTHER THOUGHT:

- How should the fact that God's grace extended even to people in Old Testament times fill us with a greater confidence to ask for His mercy today?

- How should Christ's sacrifice for our sins change our attitude toward sin?

PRAYER STARTER:

Unchanging God, even though I deserve Your punishment, I know You've extended Your grace. So I'm grasping this promise today, begging You to forgive my sins.

GOD'S CIRCLE OF LIFE

"Give us this day our daily bread. And forgive us our debts, as we forgive our debtors."
MATTHEW 6:11–12

In this section of Jesus' model prayer for believers around the world, two indisputable needs are mentioned: food and forgiveness. By putting these two needs side-by-side, Jesus illustrated just how serious the issue of salvation is. Just as a person perishes without food, so a soul will perish without God's mercy.

But how often do Christians treat forgiveness like an added perk and not a necessity? How often do we fail to repent after transgressing God's law. . .or fail to forgive someone else after that person has transgressed against us? Forgiveness is God's circle of life—if the chain is broken at any point, the soul quickly begins to wither and die. We must forgive before we can obtain forgiveness, and God's forgiveness then compels us to forgive even more.

So the next time someone wrongs you—whether it's through a harsh word or harmful action—don't give in to your desire for retaliation. Doing so will only break the cycle that keeps your soul alive. Instead, ask God for the strength to forgive that person, and then do it. That way, the next time you fall before your all-forgiving Maker in humble repentance, there will be no stain on your soul—no barrier between you and God—that might prevent Him from answering your plea.

FOR FURTHER THOUGHT:

- Why is holding a grudge against someone unbiblical?

- When you have held a grudge against someone in the past, how did it affect your relationship with God?

PRAYER STARTER:

Lord, forgive me for being unforgiving at times. Teach me to show the same mercy You've shown time and again toward me.

WHERE SHAME ENDS

O my God, I am ashamed and blush to lift up my face to You, my God. For our iniquities have increased over our head and our guilt has grown up to the heavens.

EZRA 9:6

Nobody likes to feel ashamed. Shame is one of those emotions that modern culture tries its best to remove. New forms of medicines and therapy are developed and employed each day, with varying success, in the fight against shame. Shame is treated like a weed that must be trimmed, uprooted, and cast into the furnace of history—an embarrassing relic of our supposedly less-evolved ancestors.

Sometimes, especially in cases in which a person is truly innocent yet struggles with self-doubt and depression, such treatments are beneficial—a gift from God, even. But other times, as Ezra's prayer shows, shame is not just permissible but necessary. This is shame directed toward the ugly sins that eat away at our consciences. Paul calls this shame "godly sorrow" (2 Corinthians 7:10), and despite how agonizing it feels at the time, this emotion is the sinner's best friend.

49

Why? Because it leads him to the one place where such shame can be taken away forever: the throne of God.

The next time you feel ashamed, don't ignore it or try to make it go away. Instead, bring it to God, imploring Him to forgive you for whatever stings your conscience. And then. . .leave that shame at His feet, trusting in His power to forgive and forget.

FOR FURTHER THOUGHT:

- How can a Christian man tell the difference between "godly sorrow" and unhealthy, persistent shame?

- What steps might he take to alleviate the latter?

PRAYER STARTER:

Lord, I don't want to become desensitized to sin. Please let me know when I need to confess, and then teach me how to move on.

YOUTHFUL INDISCRETIONS

*Do not remember the sins of my youth or
my transgressions. According to Your mercy
remember me for Your goodness' sake, O LORD.*
PSALM 25:7

David knew what it was like to experience the heated passions of youth. . .and the consequences that came along with them. After slaying a giant, escaping a bloodthirsty king, and finally obtaining the crown for himself, David's ego and lack of restraint led to his committing adultery and murder in one fell swoop. He sinned grievously and paid a tremendous price. And now, presumably in his old age, David begged God not to remember these sins.

We can all sympathize with David's plight. When many of us look back at the mistakes we made while young, it's tempting to cringe in embarrassment and shame. Regret lures us in like a siren's call, greedily waiting to ensnare us in its cycle of guilt and shame. And once it has us, it's impossible to escape without some serious help from above.

But God's forgiveness is greater than our guilt. When we're truly sorry for what we've done and express a desire to turn from our old ways, God forgets our sins—removing them as far as the east is from the west (Psalm 103:12). Our youthful indiscretions don't have to keep us up at night: they're forever covered by God's infinite mercy.

FOR FURTHER THOUGHT:

- How has regret over past sins ensnared you in guilt and shame?
- How might dwelling too long on youthful indiscretions inadvertently cause a relapse?

PRAYER STARTER:

God, forgive me for the sins I committed in ignorance and rebellion. Thank You for removing the guilt I felt over these decisions.

TILL THE BITTER END

"I have uttered what I do not understand, things too wonderful for me, which I do not know. . . . Therefore, I hate myself and repent in dust and ashes."

JOB 42:3, 6

Are you one of those men who hate to admit when they're wrong? Maybe you've gotten into an argument—with your wife, a coworker, a friend, or even a total stranger on social media—and it quickly became obvious that the other person had the upper ground, factually speaking. But instead of saying, "Oh. . .it looks like you're right," you buckled down and fought till the bitter end.

Don't worry—we've all been there. It's just human nature to want a victory, even if it means speaking words we don't really mean. But the moment we give in to that temptation, what was once a benign conversation immediately transforms into an ugly struggle for dominance between the forces of pride and truth.

As fallen, sinful humans, we're often tempted to kick against God's grace—to go down swinging in a fight that's impossible to win. When God tells us we need His forgiveness, we'd sometimes rather die than admit He's right. But Job understood that God's mercy isn't our enemy—it's the greatest gift we could ever receive. Even better, it's entirely free. The only thing we have to do is speak those oh-so-difficult words, "I have uttered what I do not understand. Please forgive me."

FOR FURTHER THOUGHT:

- In what ways have you spoken out of turn in the past, uttering things you do not understand?

- How can we train our minds to embrace humility each time we stumble?

PRAYER STARTER:

I made a mistake, God—there's no use in trying to hide it. Please grant me Your forgiveness so that I can start afresh.

ZEROS

"Woe is me! For I am undone because I am a man of unclean lips, and I dwell in the midst of a people of unclean lips, for my eyes have seen the King, the Lord of hosts."

ISAIAH 6:5

On a scale of one to ten, how righteous would you say you are? Maybe you give to charity on a regular basis, help that old lady cross the street sometimes, never swear, and try your best not to gossip, even when you know a story you'd *really* like to share. So. . .maybe an eight? Nine perhaps?

Bad news. You're not even close.

Having come face-to-face with God Almighty, Isaiah suddenly realized a frightening truth: on God's scale of righteousness, we're all zeros. No matter how many good deeds we do or how hard we try to avoid sin, we can't approach God's infinite holiness. We're like ants crossing a table and thinking we've traveled the universe. We haven't. Even the godliest man among us is nothing more than "a man of unclean lips." Our righteousness is but "filthy rags" (Isaiah 64:6), destined for the trash heap.

But wait—there's good news. When we pray for forgiveness, God no longer sees our righteousness (or lack thereof). Instead, because of Jesus' sacrifice, He only sees the perfect righteousness of His Son. That's why we can "come boldly to the throne of grace" (Hebrews 4:16), trusting not in our own holiness but in the one who washes us white as snow (Isaiah 1:18).

FOR FURTHER THOUGHT:

- Why do you think it's often easier for us to try to earn God's grace than to simply accept it?

- How can a Christian man overcome this dangerous impulse?

PRAYER STARTER:

Infinitely holy God, You alone are perfect, and I won't even try to pretend that my own efforts come close. Please wash away my sins. Your mercy is my only hope.

PRAYERS FOR
WISDOM

A WISDOM-BRINGING PERSPECTIVE

So teach us to number our days, that we may apply our hearts to wisdom.
PSALM 90:12

The book of Psalms is known for being poetic, but today's psalm may be the most poignant of them all. In verse 4, the psalmist tells God, "A thousand years in Your sight are but as yesterday when it is past." And then, after describing the mind-boggling infinitude of God's standard of measurement, he shifts his attention to a human life, which "is soon cut off, and we fly away" (verse 10).

So how does this line of thought lead to wisdom? By forcing us to recognize our placement in God's ultimate plan.

It's easy to become so wrapped up in our own efforts to please God that we start feeling like the hero of our own story. Humility soon gives way to arrogance, and a humble recognition of our own limitations is replaced with a false sense of immortality. In order for a Christian man to thrive, his soul needs to be a fertile ground for wisdom to take root. . .but this insidious form of pride is nothing short of poison. Obviously, God doesn't want us to belittle ourselves or fail to recognize our worth in His eyes—He merely wants us to have a proper perspective.

So when you pray today, begin by recognizing God's sovereign wisdom. Don't use your time with Him as an excuse to brag about your own efforts; instead, use it as an opportunity to let His efforts flow through you.

FOR FURTHER THOUGHT:

- When you've tried to please God in the past, how tempted were you to approach Him with a false sense of humility (bragging about your efforts rather than confessing your sin)?

- How does a proper perspective on life bring about godly fear?

PRAYER STARTER:

Father God, You are infinite, mighty, and beyond my comprehension. Teach me wisdom by helping me understand my placement in Your will.

EXPLANATION NEEDED

"Declare to us the parable of the weeds of the field."
MATTHEW 13:36

While reading a particular Bible passage, have you ever found yourself thinking, *This all sounds good...but what on earth does it mean?* Maybe it's an obscure verse in Leviticus that sends your brain in a tailspin, or perhaps it's an entire book—like Revelation or Daniel—that seems indecipherable.

Well, the disciples had the same problem. Jesus often spoke in parables—some being easier to understand than others. Often, some in His audience would walk away confused, not knowing the message He tried to convey and perhaps a bit afraid to ask (Matthew 13:13). But the disciples, recognizing that Jesus never said anything without value, were eager to ask Him to reveal the meaning of His parables to them. After all, there was no way they could learn from their Master if they didn't understand His teachings.

God wants us to study His Word with every tool He's given us—using everything from Bible dictionaries to lexicons to atlases to commentaries. But without praying for Him to open our eyes, we might as well be trying to understand a language we've never studied. Only He can impart the wisdom we need to grasp the finer points of His Word, so why would we hesitate to ask?

FOR FURTHER THOUGHT:

- What parts of the Bible do you understand the least?

- When was the last time you prayed for wisdom while reading or studying these tedious or confusing sections?

PRAYER STARTER:

God, I want to always be growing in my understanding of You. Please declare to me the meaning of Your words so I can take them to heart and employ them in my life.

ABOVE ALL ELSE

"Therefore give Your servant an understanding heart to judge Your people, that I may discern between good and bad. For who is able to judge this great people of Yours?"

1 KINGS 3:9

Reading Solomon's story, most of us would say this king was one of the lucky few. After all, what other man can say he's been approached by God with the open-ended question, "What shall I give you?" (1 Kings 3:5).

At that moment, Solomon's heart probably skipped a beat as the realization of what was happening set in. Pictures of treasure, fame, and every pleasure he could ever think of desiring flashed before his eyes. But as the strobing visions of glory subsided, Solomon found only one word that withstood the flood of endless possibilities: *wisdom.*

What good was wealth if he didn't know how to use it? What good was fame if everyone thought King Solomon was a fool? What good was a pleasurable life if it lacked direction? What good was *anything* without wisdom?

Often, it's tempting to confuse our own desires with

God's. That job we've been craving, that sleek new car, that long-sought-after relationship—it's so easy to just ask God for something we desire and then get upset when our request gets denied. But Solomon understood that a request for wisdom is one request God never turns down (see James 1:5). And once we obtain wisdom, many of these other requests shrink in value as our eyes are opened to God's bigger picture.

What's your request today?

FOR FURTHER THOUGHT:

- Why do you think God gave Solomon such a rare opportunity?
- If Solomon's heart had been different, do you think God would have made this offer?

PRAYER STARTER:

God, out of all the things I want today, there's only one thing I need—the wisdom to develop a closer walk with You. Teach me how to crave wisdom above all else.

JUST MAKING SURE

"Behold, I will put a fleece of wool on the threshing floor, and if the dew is on the fleece only, and it is dry on all the earth beside it, then I shall know that You will save Israel by my hand, as You have said."
JUDGES 6:37

Gideon is perhaps one of the most relatable people in the Bible. He was just an ordinary man, going about his ordinary, day-to-day business, when God gave him a very extraordinary task: free the Israelites from Midian. His response was a very humble—and very human—"I'm willing, Lord. . .but first, I need to be sure."

Gideon knew that God was able to use him, but he also knew his own mind could sometimes play tricks on him. *What if I just imagined the angel?* he may have thought. *What if delusions of grandeur are getting the best of me?* So by asking for wisdom—which, in this case, took the form of a physical sign—Gideon made sure he carried out God's will.

If you think God is calling you to do something, don't hesitate to ask for the wisdom to know if it's really Him. As long as your heart is truly open to performing His will, He'll be more than happy to set you on the right path.

FOR FURTHER THOUGHT:

- How was Gideon's response to God's calling different from Moses'?

- Why are we sometimes hesitant to accept God's direction in our lives?

PRAYER STARTER:

Lord, I'm willing to go where You lead. . .but first, I need to make sure it's really You who's doing the leading. Give me the wisdom to discern Your calling from my own desires.

BEFORE YOU ACT. . .

And David inquired of the LORD, saying, "Shall I pursue this troop? Shall I overtake them?"
1 SAMUEL 30:8

Many men are experts in the art of action. Whenever they have an idea or goal for the future, they leap at the chance to see it fulfilled. But how many men are experts at asking for approval?

Today's prayer shows that David understood the importance of getting the green light from God. When the Amalekites burned the city of Ziklag and captured its inhabitants (which included two of David's wives), David itched to hunt down those scoundrels and give them what they deserved. But David understood an important truth: emotions are never a reliable guide for one's life. So before he even took a step toward the enemy, David took the time to ask for God's permission.

Psalm 127:1 says, "Unless the LORD builds the house, those who build it labor in vain." So why are so many Christians hesitant to ask for God's advice? How irrational it is for a man to plow ahead without making sure his plan has been approved by the only one who can enable him to do it. Failing to ask for God's approval not only displays a lack of wisdom but betrays a man's disproportionate confidence in his own abilities and understanding. He's like an inexperienced builder tossing his employer's blueprint and choosing to make it up as he goes along.

Today, ask for God's wisdom before you act. . .and then obey whatever instructions He provides.

FOR FURTHER THOUGHT:

- In what ways have you experienced the consequences of failing to ask for God's approval?
- How might this bad memory serve as a reminder of God's perfect knowledge?

PRAYER STARTER:

Father, there's a fork in the road ahead, and I don't have a clue about which path to choose. I need Your wisdom to guide me in the right direction.

COURSE CORRECTION

"Lord, what do You want me to do?"
Acts 9:6

Imagine being in Saul's shoes. You've spent your whole life fervently following what you think is the truth, even to the point of silencing anyone who disagrees. But there's only one problem: you find out you're wrong.

Suddenly, with a flash of light and a booming voice from the sky, God Himself speaks directly to you, shattering your entire worldview with a single sentence: "I am Jesus, whom you are persecuting" (Acts 9:5). Fear blends with bafflement as you fall to your knees, a broken mess of fear and regret. "Lord," you exclaim, "what do You want me to do?"

While few men have experienced God's voice as clearly as Saul (later known as Paul) did, the emotions he felt that day are common to us all. That moment when we realize the extent of our mistakes can be a shock to our senses—a very unwanted wake-up call that forces us to rethink our decisions and reevaluate our priorities.

But rather than give in to despair, the truly penitent man can learn much from Saul's short but desperate prayer. By recognizing the error of his ways, Saul was free to ask God to show him a better way. By admitting his own limitations, Saul opened himself up to God's unlimited wisdom.

Do you need a course correction today? Have your efforts to improve or give meaning to your life been in vain? If so, maybe it's time to kneel before God with the burning question on your lips: "Lord, what do you want me to do?"

FOR FURTHER THOUGHT:

- When was the last time God corrected your erroneous understanding of some spiritual reality?
- Why do you think God often waits until we ask Him what to do before telling us what to do?

PRAYER STARTER:

Lord God, I thought I could do it alone,
but I can't. Please show me what to do next.
I surrender my plans to Your perfect will.

COMMUNICATING GOD'S NAME

"Behold, when I come to the children of Israel and shall say to them, 'The God of your fathers has sent me to you,' and they shall say to me, 'What is His name?' what shall I say to them?"

EXODUS 3:13

When God asked Moses to be the instrument by which He would free the Israelites, Moses was understandably confused. But even though he displayed a lack of faith by refusing to go at first, his prayer in today's verse sets a fantastic example for Christian men today.

In this increasingly postmodern, post-Christian culture, the gospel message seems harder and harder to convey. It's not that people don't want to hear it—instead, their worldview has become so fundamentally different from the truth found in God's Word that it's nearly impossible for them to even understand it, let alone obey it. To them, "God" is little more than an abstract concept—or even worse, a meaningless word they mutter when upset.

Frustrated by his culture's increasingly alien nature, a Christian man may feel tempted to cower in fear, unwilling to admit his faith in public. Obviously, God isn't pleased with such a response. Instead, a true man of God should pray for the wisdom to reach his ever-darkening culture—if not with arguments, then with actions and love. Just as God knew what Moses should say to the Israelites, He knows what you should say to the unbelievers you meet.

So today, ask God how you can best communicate His name.

FOR FURTHER THOUGHT:

- If Moses had tried communicating God's truth using his own wisdom, how do you think his story—and the story of all the Israelites—would have ended?

- How fearful are you of engaging the culture with the gospel message?

PRAYER STARTER:

Lord, I want to tell people about You, but I'm not sure what words I should say. I need Your Spirit to guide me as I attempt to spread Your message.

PATIENT AND WISE

Show me Your ways, O LORD. Teach me Your paths. Lead me in Your truth, and teach me, for You are the God of my salvation. On You I wait all day long.
PSALM 25:4–5

Perhaps you've heard the expression, "Be careful about praying for patience because God just might give it to you." This saying refers to the fact that patience isn't a magical gift or superpower—it must be learned. And the only way to learn patience? You guessed it—by going through situations in which you have to use it.

As today's prayer shows, patience and wisdom are two sides of the same coin. In order to know God's path, a Christian man often has to wait on God's timing. When we pray, "Lead me," we often imagine God swooping in and grabbing our hand, pulling us to a brighter future. We don't realize that "Lead me" is the same prayer as "Teach me"—a process that sounds a lot less appealing.

Maybe you're confident that God wants you to pursue a certain ministry or career, but you're not sure why it's taking so long. If so, maybe it's time to ask God for the wisdom to be patient. . .or the patience to be wise. Maybe you're just not ready for that path yet. . .or

73

maybe you're *too* ready, trying to hurry things along at a faster pace than the one God has set.

Either way, take some time today to slow down and pray for the direction and timing that only God can provide.

FOR FURTHER THOUGHT:

- Can a Christian possess wisdom without patience, or vice versa?
- Why is it necessary for Christian men to have both?

PRAYER STARTER:

Make me patient and wise, God.
Teach me how to learn from You.

ARBITRARY CHOICES

"You, Lord, who know the hearts of all men,
show which of these two You have chosen, that
he may take part in this ministry and apostleship
from which Judas fell by transgression,
that he might go to his own place."
ACTS 1:24–25

As Jesus' disciples recovered from the shock they'd experienced in recent days, they were soon faced with a troubling fork in the road. Judas' absence had left a cavity in the group that needed to be filled, and they'd narrowed their options to Joseph and Matthias.

Their next choice seemed entirely arbitrary. Both men were equally qualified; the only way to make a final decision was to draw lots—the ancient equivalent of a coin toss.

But the disciples knew this decision shouldn't be made so flippantly. So they prayed: "Show which of these two You have chosen." And then, once they were sure God had heard their prayer, they cast lots, trusting providence to guide the process of chance.

Our lives consist of a near-infinite series of small decisions. Every minute, we're faced with a dizzying array of trivial choices that come together to form who we are. There's simply no way we can make the right choice every time. . .not without God's help, that is. So when we pray for wisdom, it's not just for big, life-altering choices at the crossroads of good and evil; it's also for the small, everyday decisions we don't even realize we're making.

By asking God to guide us in all things, big and small, our lives will slowly conform to His master plan.

FOR FURTHER THOUGHT:

- How often should a Christian take his decisions, big and small, to the Lord?
- After asking God for guidance, how willing are you to trust His providence with the outcome?

PRAYER STARTER:

Father, guide my steps today. Lead me away from harmful paths, even the ones I don't recognize as such.

TOUGH QUESTION, TOUGHER ANSWER

"Shall I go up again to battle against the children of Benjamin my brother?"
Judges 20:22

The nation of Israel was faced with an impossible choice: to fight against one of its own tribes or let wickedness run unfettered through the land. Shocked by Benjamin's betrayal, hurt that things had to come to this point, the people of Israel made the only wise decision: to pray for God's wisdom. And much to their dismay, God's answer came through loud and clear: "Go up against him" (Judges 20:22).

Now, God isn't going to call you to wage actual war against anyone—Israel's case was rare and highly specific. But what about when He calls you to publicly stand up for what's right? To confront a dear friend about a sin you see in his life? To say no to an enticing offer, thus risking your relationship with that person? You know full well that a conflict may ensue, but all other options seem exhausted. In these moments of tension, we must fall before God, begging for His wisdom. And even when we don't like His answer, we must still obey, trusting in His master plan.

Sometimes, the answers we fear the most are the ones we need the most. Are you asking the right questions today?

FOR FURTHER THOUGHT:

- When was the last time you asked God what to do and were troubled by His answer?
- How did that story end?

PRAYER STARTER:

Father, I'm asking for Your wisdom, knowing that it may very well be something I don't want to hear. But even if that's the case, I'm still committed to obeying Your command.

PRAY FIRST, TALK SECOND

Then the king said to me, "What do you request?" So I prayed to the God of heaven.
NEHEMIAH 2:4

Today's prayer is unlike many others in this book, in that we don't know what Nehemiah actually prayed. But judging from the context, we can get a pretty good idea.

Upon learning that Jerusalem was in ruins, Nehemiah—who was the king's cupbearer—couldn't hide his sadness from the king. When the king asked Nehemiah what was wrong, Nehemiah held nothing back. In response, the king asked, "What do you request?"

Nehemiah was terrified. One wrong word, and he risked disrespecting the king. . .and ensuring a quick punishment for himself. If that happened, all hopes for Jerusalem's restoration would be lost. But at the same time, he couldn't just stay silent. This was his chance to make sure God's city stood in honor once again.

So he prayed. . .and God heard him.

When we think of prayer, we often think of kneeling on the ground or bowing our heads, but today's verse proves that these conditions aren't always necessary.

In fact, it shows that Nehemiah had developed such a close relationship with God that prayer was his immediate reaction whenever he needed wisdom. He had learned to pray on his feet.

What about you? When you're in the middle of a conversation (or some other activity that requires full attention) and are suddenly faced with a split-second decision, what's your first response? To try fumbling through it on your own? Or to shoot up a quick "Help me!" to the God who's always listening?

FOR FURTHER THOUGHT:

- Why do you think God places no restrictions on where and when we can pray?

- How often do you take advantage of this freedom?

PRAYER STARTER:

Lord, may there always be a prayer waiting on my lips whenever I need Your wisdom. Teach me how to pray first and talk second.

JUST A CHILD

"Ah, Lord GOD! Behold, I cannot speak, for I am a child."
JEREMIAH 1:6

How would you react if God directly told you that you were destined to change the world? Would you feel honored and excited, eager to take on the challenge? Or would you feel paralyzed with fear, unable to imagine yourself handling such a monumental task?

Jeremiah had the second reaction. But while today's prayer might make him come across as cowardly or lacking in faith, a closer look reveals an attitude that all Christian men should have.

"I cannot speak," Jeremiah rightfully said. Rightfully, because there was no way he could fulfill his calling on his own. By recognizing his own limitations, Jeremiah took the first step toward allowing God's power to work through him.

"I am a child," he truthfully claimed. But to whom does a child turn whenever he stumbles upon a problem he can't solve? That's right—his father. Jeremiah understood that without God to guide him as only a loving Father could, he was just a child lost in the forest.

Whenever we're faced with the immensity of God's calling for us—whether it's a missionary trip around the world or simply a holy, obedient life—it's tempting to either scoff at the seeming impossibility of it all or to overestimate our own abilities. But as Jeremiah's response shows, neither attitude is correct. When we choose to answer God's call, our reply should be, "I don't know how, Lord. But I know You do."

Only then can a Christian man change the world.

FOR FURTHER THOUGHT:

- At what point does self-confidence cross the line into pride?

- How can a Christian man prevent this transition from happening?

PRAYER STARTER:

Father, only You know the way forward. Please shine Your light on the path ahead so I can accomplish all the amazing things You've created me to do.

STUMPED

"The people whom I am among are six hundred thousand footmen, and You have said, 'I will give them meat, that they may eat a whole month.' Shall the flocks and the herds be slain for them, to satisfy them? Or shall all the fish of the sea be gathered together for them, to satisfy them?"
NUMBERS 11:21–22

Moses wasn't exactly the most willing participant in God's plan. Having been called to travel to a place he didn't want to go, speak to a man he didn't want to see, and lead a people he didn't want to lead, Moses had to gradually learn the art of obedience and trust.

Today's scripture shows he still had a bit to learn. Even after he'd seen God sling plagues from the heavens and split the Red Sea into halves, Moses was still caught up on statistics. With only the slightest touch of cynicism in his voice, he asked God how in the world He expected him to pull this off. There were just too many mouths to feed!

God answered him, of course, and brought about a solution that nobody saw coming—quail swept in by the wind (Numbers 11:31).

When you feel God is calling you to do something that seems impossible, don't be afraid to ask Him for the wisdom to do it. In fact, this is just what He wants His children to do. But don't be too surprised if He responds, "You don't have to do anything. Just sit back and watch Me work."

FOR FURTHER THOUGHT:

- Why do you think God kept answering Moses' prayers, despite his occasional lack of faith?
- How are we, as modern Christian men, any different than Moses who seemed doubtful?

PRAYER STARTER:

All-knowing God, I'm stumped. I just can't see a way forward on this path You've called me to take. Show me what to do next.

DESTINED FOR GREATNESS

*"O my Lord, let the man of God whom You
sent come again to us and teach us what we
shall do for the child who shall be born."*
JUDGES 13:8

Manoah's world was one marked with pain and disappointment. His nation had been oppressed by the
Philistines for forty years, and his wife was unable to
bear children. Stories of past miracles seemed trite and
out of fashion. He and his wife had resigned themselves
to a childless, hopeless future.

But that's when God showed up.

"You shall conceive and bear a son," an angel told
Manoah's wife (Joshua 13:3), who was no doubt paralyzed with a mixture of excitement and fear. And not
only that but this child would "begin to deliver Israel
out of the hand of the Philistines" (13:5). Manoah knew
a monumental task lay before him. His child was destined for greatness. . .and God handed him the keys to
his safety and growth.

Maybe you don't have kids yet, but you're con-
sidering the prospect of raising a family someday. Or
maybe you do, and you're finding out it's a lot harder

than you thought. Either way, let Manoah's prayer be your guide. Ask God for the wisdom to raise your children right—to bring them up as lights that will pierce the darkness in their corner of the world. They may never be elected to public office or even featured on television, but they can be spiritual freedom fighters for the kingdom of God.

All it takes is a wise father who's willing to learn and teach God's wisdom.

FOR FURTHER THOUGHT:

- How attentive are you to your children and the gifts God has given them?
- How can you develop a love and trust for God so they can be shining lights for Christ?

PRAYER STARTER:

Father, lead me in Your wisdom so I will be able to lead children of my own.

INHUMAN WISDOM

Then Daniel went to his house and made the matter known to Hananiah, Mishael, and Azariah, his companions, that they would ask mercies of the God of heaven concerning this secret, that Daniel and his companions should not perish with the rest of the wise men of Babylon.

DANIEL 2:17–18

The Bible makes it abundantly clear that Daniel was a very wise man, even capable of interpreting dreams when necessary (Daniel 1:17, 20). In fact, he was so wise that the prophet Ezekiel used him as the gold standard for wisdom (Ezekiel 28:3). But what was the source of Daniel's wisdom? Was he just a sharp guy with lots of book knowledge or street smarts?

Today's passage would suggest otherwise. On his own, Daniel was just like any other man. But because he had a close relationship with God, coming to Him in prayer each time a need arose, his wisdom was unmatched throughout the Babylonian kingdom. This wisdom was divinely imparted, not learned.

While few of us will have the ability to interpret dreams or gain an audience with kings, we can still access the deep storehouses of God's wisdom through prayer. God hasn't changed a bit since Daniel's day, so He's still willing to impart His guidance to anyone willing to receive it.

Today, feel free to ask God for the wisdom to face every challenge that life throws at you. As you grow in your walk with Him, you'll find yourself becoming more and more like Daniel each day.

FOR FURTHER THOUGHT:

- In what ways was Daniel's God-given wisdom fundamentally different from human wisdom?
- How can you reframe your prayers to focus more on gaining godly wisdom?

PRAYER STARTER:

Lord, there are some things in life that I just can't know—and probably never will. But I realize You're able to reveal to me everything I need to know in my walk with You. Please grow my wisdom today.

PRAYERS FOR DELIVERANCE

AN UNDESERVED RESCUE

"Lord, save me!"
MATTHEW 14:30

We all know the story. Peter sees Jesus walking on the water, and asks to join Him. Jesus says, "Come," so Peter gets out of the boat and starts stepping on the waves himself. But when he notices the wind, he gets frightened and starts to sink, crying out the immortal words of today's prayer.

Countless sermons have focused entirely on Peter's lack of faith. . .while others have rightly pointed out the immense faith that Peter must have had to even start walking on the water. But the crux of the story—the one thing that made the difference between life and death—was Peter's short, concise prayer as his feet slipped beneath the foam.

This prayer is the embodiment of humility. Nowhere in Peter's voice is there a sense of "Why is this happening to me?" or "I tried the best I could!" Instead, all we hear is a humble recognition of his own helplessness in the face of certain death. For Peter, Jesus was the ultimate protector—the only one capable of pulling him from the angry waves.

When we make mistakes, carelessly slipping into sin only to realize it once we're waist deep, our only hope for redemption lies in Jesus. The more we struggle on our own, the more our sin behaves like quicksand, dragging us down toward death. But by reaching our hand out to God—trusting entirely in His mercy—and allowing Him to pull us out, we can find the same deliverance Peter found that day on the Sea of Galilee.

FOR FURTHER THOUGHT:

- When was the last time you found yourself caught in sin?
- What was your response?
- How did you finally escape?

PRAYER STARTER:

Save me, Lord! I don't deserve Your help, but I need it now more than ever.

OUTNUMBERED AND OUTGUNNED

*You are my hiding place. You shall preserve
me from trouble. You shall surround
me with songs of deliverance.*

PSALM 32:7

Today's prayer was written by David, a man who was all too familiar with being outnumbered and outgunned. When King Saul was alive, David spent his time hiding in the mountains and caves. He did have his followers, but they were few in comparison to the king's. David had to rely on God to protect him.

Perhaps this psalm was composed during one of these times—the brilliant poet-shepherd, crouched fearfully in a rock's crevice, scribbling his desperate prayer on a sheet of tear-soaked papyrus. As the sounds of Saul's army drew closer, the words in today's verse flew from his fingers: "You are my hiding place. You shall preserve me from trouble."

What a moving depiction of our walk with God. Most western Christian men aren't literally on the run, fleeing a physical enemy bent on ending their lives. But how often do we find ourselves in a spiritual cave, surrounded by the dark whispers of doubt, anger, bitterness, and despair? As the armies of sin and hopelessness close in, we realize that our only hope—our one chance for survival—lies in the rescuing power of God.

When God is your hiding place, even the most determined forces of darkness will never be able to find you.

FOR FURTHER THOUGHT:

- Why do you think God sometimes lets us experience the feeling of being outnumbered?
- What would our spiritual lives look like if God solved every problem before we became aware of it?

PRAYER STARTER:

Father God, I'm here again—surrounded by the enemy with no way out. It'll take a miracle to get me out this time. . .but I know that's just what You specialize in.

WEAK AND WEARY

"Sir, I have no man to put me into the pool when the water is troubled. But while I am coming, another steps down before me."
JOHN 5:7

This crippled man had spent his days in anticipation, patiently waiting for an angel to trouble the waters, imbuing them with healing properties (verse 4). But each time the waters began to stir—each time the man's eyes lit up with the joy of expectation as he feebly crawled toward the pool—another person strode past him and plunged in, shattering his hopes.

But then Jesus came along.

When Jesus asked him, "Do you want to be healed?" (John 5:6), the man at first thought Jesus asked about his ability to walk down into the pool. The weariness in his reply is more than evident—even the word "Sir" is laden with a sense of frustration and disappointment.

So imagine his surprise when Jesus responded, "Rise, take up your bed, and walk" (verse 8). Suddenly, years of weariness dissolved into joy as, with newly capable legs, the man stood up for the first time in his life. A miracle had taken place that day. . .and neither the pool nor the man's efforts to climb in had anything to do with it.

Do you feel trapped by your circumstances or by a sinful habit, forever searching but failing to find an escape route? Today, Jesus is walking your way. Go to Him with your weariness and stop trying to climb out yourself. Just let Him take your hand and bring you to your feet.

FOR FURTHER THOUGHT:

- Why do you think Jesus asked the man if he wanted to be healed?

- How does the man's depressed reply show that he was on the right path toward faith?

PRAYER STARTER:

I've tried so hard, Lord, but I just can't pull myself out of this pit. I need You to reach down Your hand today.

KEPT FROM EVIL

"Oh that You would bless me indeed, and enlarge my territory, and that Your hand might be with me, and that You would keep me from evil, that it may not grieve me!"

1 CHRONICLES 4:10

"Keep me from evil, that it may not grieve me." Although we don't know much about Jabez, the man who spoke today's prayer, these words reveal two important truths.

First, Jabez realized the journey ahead would be filled with challenges and danger. His life was one of war and conquest—an endless battle against the pagan, wicked forces that stood in his way. He knew he would face countless enemies as he pressed forward, and some of them would be far beyond his ability to overcome.

But second, Jabez knew that God could deliver him. As long as God remained by his side, not a single spear could pierce his armor. Defeat was impossible; victory was his for the taking.

Imagine if we all had the courage and faith of Jabez. To ask for deliverance before the problem arises. . .and then to plunge headlong into battle with the forces of darkness, knowing God would shield us from meeting a dishonorable end.

Today, don't be afraid to ask God to deliver you from evil, even if the evil hasn't yet arrived. Often, our lives are a continual barrage of struggles against the enemy of our souls. Battle is coming—but in Jesus, you are protected.

FOR FURTHER THOUGHT:

- What do you need deliverance from?
- How does Jabez's extreme confidence differ from the overconfidence that God's enemies often display?

PRAYER STARTER:

Almighty God, I'm not sure what tomorrow holds. It may be peaceful. . .or it may hold the darkest struggle I've ever faced. Whatever the case, I know You can bring me through.

FOR GOD'S GLORY

"Truly, Lord, the kings of Assyria have destroyed the nations and their lands and have cast their gods into the fire. . . . Now therefore, O Lord our God, I beseech You: save us out of his hand, that all the kingdoms of the earth may know that You alone are the Lord God."
2 Kings 19:17-18, 19

When praying for deliverance, it's sometimes easy to fall into a selfish mindset—an attitude of, "Lord, I don't like this situation I'm in right now. . .so get me out!" But today's prayer, spoken by Hezekiah as the Assyrian army closed in on Jerusalem, illustrates the correct way a man of God should approach his Creator in times of distress.

Instead of focusing on how badly his city would suffer if the Assyrians succeeded, Hezekiah focused on the integrity of God's character in the eyes of the world. The only thing worse than being killed by a savage army, Hezekiah realized, would be to watch as God's name was disrespected, placed on the same level as idols of wood and stone.

This was the fear that kept Hezekiah awake at

night—the fear that prompted him to pray desperately for the salvation of his nation. And because God knew Hezekiah's heart, He listened to this prayer, sending an angel to demolish the Assyrian army that night.

Clearly, there's nothing wrong with praying for our own protection. But we mustn't forget that our ultimate goal should always be to show God's glory.

FOR FURTHER THOUGHT:

- When did you last ask God to magnify His name by rescuing you from a tough spot?
- How is God glorified through your life in the eyes of the world?

PRAYER STARTER:

God, I don't want the world to look at my life and see a failure—a hollow shell with Your name written on top. Let me triumph over the evil that besets me so that all might see how powerful You are.

"BE PLEASED"

Be pleased, O LORD, to deliver me.
O LORD, hurry to help me.
PSALM 40:13

The Psalms are filled with urgent cries for help—many, if not most, being written by David about the enemies who tried to kill him. But buried within today's prayer is an idea that reaches far beyond the urgent situation at hand: the desire to find God's approval.

"Be pleased, O LORD, to deliver me," David wrote. Understanding that he was a sinful man, David begged God for mercy. "I know I'm not worthy, God," he seems to be saying, "but may there be something in my life that grabs Your attention and causes You to pull me from this awful pit." Obviously, David knew that his own efforts just wouldn't cut it—it was only by the grace of God that rescue would come. And that's exactly what he asked for.

As Christians, we know that the one thing that always garners God's approval is faith in His Son, Jesus Christ. Without it, there's no reason to expect God to save us. But even then, faith is a gift that comes directly from God Himself. So where does that leave us? At His feet, begging Him, "Be pleased, O LORD, to deliver me."

Thankfully, the Lord *is* pleased to deliver us—to grant us not only the faith to ask Him but the salvation we so desperately need. Because of God's grace, help is always on the way.

FOR FURTHER THOUGHT:

- How often have you tried to "convince" God to rescue you by doing more good works?

- Why is this never a good strategy?

PRAYER STARTER:

Father God, You're the only one who can rescue me from the evils and dangers I face each day. Please extend Your mercy to me and protect my life today.

SURPRISE!

"If You are willing, You can make me clean."
MARK 1:40

In Jesus' day, leprosy was no joke. Contracting this often fatal skin disease meant resigning yourself to a life of exclusion, cut off from the company of your friends and loved ones. The wife you kissed, the children you hugged, the parents you cared for—all these relationships, gone in an instant. You were no longer able to even touch them. Nothing would ever be the same.

That's the terrifying situation in which the man who prayed today's scripture found himself. But having heard of Jesus' power to heal all manner of diseases, this man rightly concluded that leprosy was no different. The next verse gives the most important detail of the account: "Moved with compassion, Jesus put out His hand and *touched* him." That's right—not only did Jesus heal this man, but He did so in a way that spat in the face of the disease itself. Jesus' touch didn't ensure His own sickness—it killed the sickness altogether.

When the man asked for Jesus' help, he probably had no idea just how powerful Jesus truly was. And how could he? None of us can really grasp the immensity of God's might. All we can do is approach Him with our need for deliverance, step back, and watch Him surpass our expectations.

FOR FURTHER THOUGHT:

- How has God gone above and beyond your requests in the past?

- How has this impacted your prayer life?

PRAYER STARTER:

Lord God, I'm really worried about this challenge I'm facing right now. But I know You're more than capable of handling it. Surprise me with Your power once again.

THROUGH THE FIRE

"Father, if You are willing, remove this cup from Me. Nevertheless not My will, but Yours, be done."
LUKE 22:42

Today's prayer is perhaps one of the most devastating in the Bible. As Jesus approached His final hours, knowing a long, painful death awaited Him on the cross, the stress was so great upon Him that His sweat became drops of blood (verse 44).

In this agonizing moment of dread, Jesus' divine and human natures were both on full display. His human nature screamed, "Father, it's too much! Deliver Me!" But his divine nature—attuned to His ultimate purpose—quietly accepted His Father's will.

The fact that Jesus—God in the flesh—struggled so deeply should give us comfort. Even the embodiment of perfection cried out for deliverance...so why should we feel ashamed when the same emotions surge in our hearts? Men of God are not robots, capable of suppressing all feelings whenever it's convenient. We hurt. We get angry. We feel the sting of betrayal. We long for a better future. We cry out against the injustice we see perpetuated against others—and often against ourselves.

When the fire of pain comes, asking God to pull us out is simply human. But as we see in Jesus' prayer, our cries must always come with a disclaimer: "Your will be done." The God who sometimes sends you into the fire is the same God who's able to bring you through it. After all, it takes a fire to purify the gold.

FOR FURTHER THOUGHT:

- What would the world be like today if Jesus had only prayed the first half of this prayer?
- How has a painful event in your own life led to a good outcome?

PRAYER STARTER:

Father, deliver me from the suffering up ahead! But if that's not Your will, give me the wisdom and strength to endure.

UNSEEN DANGERS

Keep back Your servant also from presumptuous sins; let them not have dominion over me. Then I shall be upright, and I shall be innocent of the great transgression.

PSALM 19:13

You've no doubt heard the expression, "An ounce of prevention is worth a pound of cure." When you know a potentially harmful situation is coming—whether it's a thunderstorm or a financial downturn—what's the first thing you do? You start preparing, building up defenses so the coming calamity won't be as damaging as it would be if you were caught unawares.

David understood that as long as he walked with God, temptation lurked around every corner. But unlike a storm, temptation can't be accurately predicted. . .so David prayed to be on his toes. Not only that, but he prayed for deliverance before the chance to sin even came. On his own, he realized he was powerless to fend off sin's enticing glow—a hard fact proved true by his terrible failure with Bathsheba.

How often do you pray for God to deliver you from sin? Are you constantly aware of the possibility that tomorrow may bring a struggle, or do you prefer to treat temptation half-heartedly, content to cross that bridge when you get to it? Such carelessness will sabotage your Christian walk if you let it. So today, be sure to cry out to the only one who can deliver you before danger comes.

FOR FURTHER THOUGHT:

- How does David's own life prove the necessity of relying on God to deliver us from sin?

- How often do you pray *before* you've been tempted to sin?

PRAYER STARTER:

Lord, things may be calm right now, but I know You've still called me to be alert for any signs of spiritual trouble. Please save me from the dangers I don't yet see.

BARGAINING WITH GOD

And Jephthah made a vow to the LORD and said,
"If You shall without fail deliver the children
of Ammon into my hands, then it shall be that
whatever comes out of the doors of my house
to meet me, when I return in peace from the
children of Ammon, shall surely be the LORD's,
and I will offer it up for a burnt offering."
JUDGES 11:30–31

Jephthah's story is one of the most tragic in the Bible. He was clearly a godly man, and to a person reading his story for the first time, it would appear that he did nothing wrong in today's prayer. But when Jephthah returned from battle, the first thing that came out of his door was not an animal. . .but his own daughter.

Naturally, this raises a question: Which decision would have been worse—to break his vow to God or, as Jephthah chose to do, commit the sin of human sacrifice? While this passage doesn't attempt to answer that conundrum, it does illustrate an important truth: we should never rashly bargain with God.

If it is truly God's will to deliver you from a bad situation, and if your heart is right with Him, then there's no need to try to cut a quick deal. When it comes to such prayers, God's currency consists of faith and honesty—there's nothing else you can offer Him that will change His mind. Just come to Him with your urgent request, sincerely believing in His ability and willingness to help, and that will be enough.

FOR FURTHER THOUGHT:

- What's the difference between making a commitment to God and bargaining with Him?
- How could Jephthah have avoided this whole dilemma?

PRAYER STARTER:

Lord, I don't want to make a promise to You that I can't keep. Thank You for making such rash vows unnecessary for gaining an audience with You.

CYCLE-BREAKING GRACE

*And the children of Israel said to the LORD,
"We have sinned. Do to us whatever seems good
to You. Only deliver us this day, we ask You."*
JUDGES 10:15

Israel's spiritual state followed a very rigid and disheartening pattern. First, they would follow God for a while, enjoying a period of peace and protection from their enemies. Then they'd rebel, resulting in their captivity for a short time. And then they'd repent, causing God to restore them to peace. . .where they began the process all over again.

Today's prayer came at the beginning of the third step. God was tired of their repeated disobedience (see Judges 10:11–14), but Israel knew He was their only chance for survival. Humble and broken before their Creator, the people collectively fell before God, freely admitting the sins of their past. God, of course, knew this wouldn't be the end of their sinful cycle, but the Bible says, "His soul was grieved for the misery of Israel" (10:16).

Maybe you've been suffering the consequences of a mistake—or series of mistakes—you made years ago.

Maybe you feel overwhelmed by guilt, unable to see how or why God would possibly deliver you from the chains of depression, addiction, or whatever else might be shackling your soul. If so, take heart: God still cares. No matter how many times you've blown it, God is still willing to wipe your slate clean and put you back on your feet. And once He does deliver you, you don't have to repeat your mistakes. He'll give you the strength to break the cycle once and for all.

FOR FURTHER THOUGHT:

- Why was Israel's humility an important part of their prayer?

- What sin has shackled your soul?

- How willing are you to repeat Israel's prayer from today's passage?

PRAYER STARTER:

Almighty Father, I regret the decisions that have led me to this place of estrangement from You. Rescue me from this horrible cycle—I never want to return here again.

A FUTURE-CHANGING PRAYER

*"I beseech You, O LORD, remember now
how I have walked before You in truth and
wholeheartedly and have done what is good
in Your sight." And Hezekiah wept sorely.*

2 KINGS 20:3

Does God ever change His mind?

That's the question many Christians ask themselves
while reading this story. Just two verses prior, God
had told Hezekiah in no uncertain terms, "Set your
house in order, for you shall die, and not live" (20:1).
Stunned by the sudden revelation, the king didn't try to
bargain for God's mercy or complain about the unfair-
ness of it all. Instead, he came before God baffled and
broken, his prayer was less of a request than a feeble
But Lord. . .why?

And that was enough.

God, in His infinite wisdom, no doubt knew the
ultimate outcome—that Hezekiah's prayer would result
in fifteen years being added to his life. So in that sense,
Hezekiah didn't change God's mind. But this king's
sincere display of humility and desperation certainly
changed his own future.

Most of us have been in Hezekiah's shoes. Faced with an incomprehensible tragedy, all we can do is fall before God, allowing the Holy Spirit to make intercession for us "with groanings that cannot be uttered" (Romans 8:26). Implicit in our prayer is a cry for deliverance, even when all hope seems lost. And sometimes, God chooses to answer no, knowing that this loss will bring about a greater gain in the future. But other times, as seen in Hezekiah's case, our prayers of desperation do bring about a change as God looks down upon us with compassion.

Even in life's darkest moments, it's never too late to pray.

FOR FURTHER THOUGHT:

- Why do you think God announced Hezekiah's impending death in the first place?

- When was the last time you felt as desperate as Hezekiah?

PRAYER STARTER:

Father, You know best. Please deliver me from suffering, but only when You see fit. I'm humbly submitting to Your will.

PRAYERS
FOR FAVOR

NO PRESSURE!

> *"O LORD God of my master Abraham, I ask You, send me success this day, and show kindness to my master, Abraham."*
>
> GENESIS 24:12

Abraham's servant, the speaker in today's verse, had been sent on a very important mission: to find a wife for Isaac, Abraham's son.

This servant had heard of God's promise to Abraham about his descendants, and he'd also undoubtedly heard of the miraculous circumstances surrounding Isaac's birth. He knew his task would not only ensure the happiness of his master's son but impact the course of entire nations.

No pressure!

Abraham's servant knew that such a monumental decision couldn't be made on a whim—it had to come about through prayer. So he got down on his knees and prayed for a very specific, already-determined sign that would point him to the right woman. This sign couldn't happen by mere chance—it had to stem from God's favor.

Have you ever been given a task with consequences

so large that you felt compelled to pray. . .and then pray even harder? Maybe it was a final exam in college or a work project that would destroy your job if you failed. Even though you might not have felt the same pressure that Abraham's servant felt, you still recognized the need for God's favor to be upon you as you navigated this minefield.

Today, don't be afraid to pray for God's assistance in any task you face—big or small. Come to Him, acknowledging your dependence on His mercy, and He will be more than happy to help.

FOR FURTHER THOUGHT:

- To whom does God show His favor?
- How might the answer to that question impact your approach to praying for help?

PRAYER STARTER:

Father, I'm sometimes afraid of what might happen in the future—that my efforts won't be enough. Grant me Your favor so I can effectively fulfill my calling.

MAKING A MOVE

*"O Lord, I implore You, let Your ear now be attentive
to the prayer of Your servant and to the prayer
of Your servants, who desire to fear Your name.
And let Your servant prosper this day, I pray You,
and grant him mercy in the sight of this man."*

NEHEMIAH 1:11

In ancient times, approaching the king for a favor was
no light thing—just look at Esther's story for proof. But
Nehemiah, the king's cupbearer, saw no other option if
he wanted to see Jerusalem restored to its former glory.
Clearly, nobody else took the initiative. Nehemiah was
just the right person for the job.

That's why Nehemiah prayed the words in today's
verse. He knew that even though he couldn't stand by
any longer, his actions would mean nothing unless God
was with him. So he prayed for favor—that his shot in
the dark would somehow find its target and result in
the rebuilding of God's holy city.

When you're presented with a golden opportunity to
change your circumstances (or someone else's), what's
your first action? To leap headlong into the fray, hoping
for the best? Or to fall to your knees, praying that God

will bestow success upon your efforts?

Nehemiah understood that behind every successful action is the seal of God's favor—a favor that can only be obtained through the prayers of His people. So today, if you see something you can do to make a difference, don't be afraid to act. But first, don't forget to pray.

FOR FURTHER THOUGHT:

- Why do you think God asks us to pray for His favor if He already knows what's best for us?

- How do prayer and action work hand in hand?

PRAYER STARTER:

All-knowing Father, sometimes it's scary to step up and work for positive change. But I sense You telling me it's time. Please bless my efforts today.

THE WRESTLING MATCH

"I will not let You go unless You bless me."
GENESIS 32:26

Today's prayer was uttered in what is one of the weird-est stories in the Bible. One night, as Jacob returned home to meet his brother Esau—who'd threatened to kill him after Jacob deceitfully stole his birthright—he encountered a stranger in the wilderness. This stranger, Jacob soon learned, was God Himself.

So what was Jacob's response? To fall down and wor-ship Him? To turn and flee, fearful of the wrath that may fall on him for his sins? Nope. Jacob wrestled with Him.

While we may never know exactly what sparked this strange decision (or why God didn't immediately paralyze him on the spot), we do know one thing: Jacob wasn't one to give up. Maybe he knew this was a once-in-a-lifetime opportunity to obtain God's favor. Or maybe Jacob, burning with guilt over his deceit toward Esau, was desperate to receive a blessing from a source other than his own cunning.

Either way, God granted Jacob his request. . .and gave him a name that would define God's chosen people for eternity: Israel.

While we'll never have the chance to face God in a wrestling match, we are free to grapple with God's promises each day through prayer. God loves to see His children determined, unwilling to give up on the blessings they know God has promised them. So the next time you feel as if your prayers are going nowhere, don't quit. Keep wrestling for God's favor.

FOR FURTHER THOUGHT:

- When was the last time you felt like you wrestled with God?

- Why do you think God sometimes wants us to go through such efforts before He grants our requests?

PRAYER STARTER:

Lord, give me the determination to take hold of Your promises and never let go, even if it means wrestling until the break of day.

MORE THAN A MOUNTAIN

Then Joshua spoke to the LORD on the day when the LORD delivered up the Amorites before the children of Israel, and he said in the sight of Israel: "Sun, stand still on Gibeon, and you, Moon, in the Valley of Aijalon."
JOSHUA 10:12

In Mark 11:23, Jesus said, "Whoever shall say to this mountain, 'Be removed and be cast into the sea,' and shall not doubt in his heart. . .he shall have whatever he says." Obviously, this is a fairly big guarantee. But today's prayer, spoken by Joshua in the heat of an intense battle, makes this promise look like an understatement. Not only did God shove aside a mountain that day, He seemingly stopped the rotation of the Earth.

How often do we as Christian men assume that God must follow our rules when He works? When we pray for God to grant us favor in a way that goes against our common experience, do we secretly end our prayers with the words, "if You can"? How certain are we of God's ability to perform miracles?

Today's prayer should clear up any confusion once and for all. If God can halt nature's progression just so His people could triumph over their enemies, He's certainly able to work all things out for good for those who love Him. The only question that remains is if we're willing to ask.

FOR FURTHER THOUGHT:

- When was the last time you prayed for God to do the impossible so His name would be glorified through you?

- How often do you end prayers by saying, "if You can"? What might this reveal about your understanding of God's nature?

PRAYER STARTER:

Almighty Father, when I look at my circumstances, sometimes they seem hopeless. Please grant me Your favor and work on my behalf so all will know the powerful God I serve.

THE SPIRITUAL WASTELAND

Restore us to Yourself, O LORD, and we shall be restored. Renew our days as of old.
LAMENTATIONS 5:21

Have you ever wished your life had a reset button? Perhaps after years of bad choices, wastefulness, and varying degrees of apathy, you've found yourself in a wasteland—spiritually, mentally, and emotionally. All that time, you'd convinced yourself this day would never come. . .but now here it was, cruelly reminding you of all the decisions that led you here.

That's where Israel had found themselves when today's prayer was written. As Jeremiah surveyed the literal wasteland left behind by the Babylonians' destruction of Jerusalem, he cried out to God in despair. Every crumbled building—every dusty, barren street—screamed the story of Israel's sin and the punishment that had followed. Now, all that was left was a bitter reminder. . .and Jeremiah's impassioned plea for restoration.

Do you need restoration today? Have you prayed for God's forgiveness but don't know how to move forward after such a big fall? If so, make Jeremiah's prayer your own. Fall before the God of second chances and tell Him your need. The change might not come immediately but rest assured: your prayer will begin the process of full restoration. Just put your broken pieces in God's hands and watch as He makes a masterpiece.

FOR FURTHER THOUGHT:

- How does the fact that Israel's captivity was eventually reversed give you hope for your future, especially when you're suffering the consequences of your own mistakes?

- What does this say about the possibility of running out of chances with God?

PRAYER STARTER:

Father God, I need Your favor in my life. Everything seems to be falling apart, and I know only You can put it all back together. Please start the process of renewal today.

THE REAL THING

"I beseech You, show me Your glory."
EXODUS 33:18

Moses' story echoes the journey of every Christian man who seeks a closer walk with his Creator. At first, Moses was terrified when God called him. But God persisted, and Moses eventually obeyed. As time passed and the evidences of God's power grew in number, Moses became more willing. Even though his faith still wavered, he learned to lean more fully on God each day. And by the time he uttered today's prayer, Moses had grown closer to God than any man alive. He'd quite literally scaled the mountain of God's grandeur and communed with his Maker through dense clouds of fire and lightning. And now, he sought the impossible: to see God's glory for himself.

What is your ultimate goal in Your walk with God? To improve your behavior? To read the Bible an extra five minutes per day? To respond to frustrations with some manner of peace? While all these are admirable aspirations, none of them should be our endgame. We must remember that our final spiritual destination is at the feet of God in heaven, struck with an eternity of awe as we finally lay our eyes on the glory of our Father.

Once we say to God, "Show me Your glory," we start striving toward *that* goal. Our spiritual walk suddenly shifts from a light stroll to the exhilarating, cliff-scaling climb it was always meant to be.

Are you willing to start scaling God's mountain today?

FOR FURTHER THOUGHT:

- How does the fact that Moses was far from perfect encourage us to keep pressing toward God's glory?

- Before reading today's devotion, how would you have described your spiritual endgame?

PRAYER STARTER:

Show me Your glory, Lord. I'm no longer content to settle for spiritual instability or a faith dependent on transitory emotions. I want the real thing.

NOT IN VAIN

*Remember me, O my God, concerning this, and
do not wipe out my good deeds that I have done
for the house of my God and for its services.*

NEHEMIAH 13:14

At first glance, Nehemiah's prayer in today's verse
might seem a little selfish. He appears to be saying,
"Remember all the good stuff I did, God? So do I. Now,
where's the reward?"

But a closer look shows that nothing could be further
from the truth. Nehemiah had just finished overseeing
the construction of Jerusalem—an act that had gained
him more than a few enemies. And now, even after the
work was complete, Nehemiah knew there would still be
dangers—both of sabotage from without and of spiritual
apathy from within (Nehemiah 13:17). Knowing his enemies' hatred and the Israelites' rebellious tendencies,
Nehemiah prayed that all his hard work would not be
in vain—that God would bestow His eternal favor upon
Nehemiah's efforts.

When we work for God—whether it's sharing the
gospel, giving to charity, or loving our enemies—it's only
natural to pray that our work is not in vain. One of the

most discouraging things in the world is to watch our biggest accomplishments for God crumble under the slightest pressure. It's not that we seek fame for what we've done—we seek only God's favor on our deeds, since that is always enough.

FOR FURTHER THOUGHT:

- When you finish a task, how quickly do you pray that God will preserve the positive results?

- How can praying a prayer similar to Nehemiah's prepare you for your own challenges from your enemies?

PRAYER STARTER:

Lord, please don't let my work for You go in vain. Once I finish the task You've called me to do, only You can make sure it lasts.

DELAYED RESPONSE

"Take vengeance on my adversary."
Luke 18:3

Okay, so this one's *technically* not a prayer. In one of Jesus' parables, a woman begs a cranky, impatient judge for justice to be served. At first, the judge ignores her, but he finally gives in and takes her case. . .for no other reason than to simply stop her nagging. Since God, Jesus says, is patient and loving, we as Christians should never give up on bringing our requests to Him. After all, He's much more likely to answer than this imperfect judge.

The content of this woman's request is less important than the fierceness and determination with which she made it. Rather than throwing in the towel after her first attempt, she kept knocking at the door of the only one who could help.

Have you ever started praying for something—a better job, a solution to a struggling relationship, salvation for a close friend—only to give up when it seemed God wasn't answering? Maybe you felt like your prayers were rubber bands, bouncing off the ceiling and falling limply to the ground. But perhaps it wasn't the quality of your prayer that was the problem—perhaps it was the fact that you stopped.

God tests our sincerity sometimes (see: Abraham and Isaac). And if we just quit praying after a couple of days, what kind of sincerity is that? Today, make an effort to push through the discouragement that often comes with unanswered prayer. Who knows? God's answer may lie behind your next request.

FOR FURTHER THOUGHT:

- Why have you been quick to stop praying for something in the past?
- Which abandoned prayers will you rekindle today?

PRAYER STARTER:

Father, I know You want to hear often from Your children. Give me a greater determination to keep praying, even if the answer doesn't come when I expect it.

CROSSING A LINE

"Grant that these two sons of mine may sit, the one on Your right hand and the other on the left, in Your kingdom."
MATTHEW 20:21

When a man prays for God's favor, it can be very easy for his prayer to step out of the bounds of humility and into a prideful sense of self-importance. What may begin as an "I need Your help, Lord" slowly evolves into a "Give me this because I deserve it." And the closer a man gets to that line, the lower the probability that God will answer his prayer.

Today's prayer sprinted across that line and never looked back.

Not only did the mother of James and John want Jesus to favor her kids above everyone else, but she also framed her request using the most audacious language imaginable. She envisioned an eternity of heaven's population worshipping at Jesus' feet. . .while her two sons sat at His side, far above the crowd, smiling down at all those "commoners" who would never reach their status.

Needless to say, Jesus was not pleased with her

prayer. "Whoever wants to be chief among you," He responded, "let him be your servant" (Matthew 20:27). When God shows favor to someone, it's not to stroke that person's ego—it's to provide grounds for a testimony that will point toward God's unmatched love.

Is that your ultimate desire today?

FOR FURTHER THOUGHT:

- How can a Christian man make sure his prayers are never motivated by pride, greed, or selfishness?

- When was the last time you checked your own heart during your prayer time?

PRAYER STARTER:

Holy God, I'm not asking to be better than anyone else. I just want You to be pleased with my life. Shine your loving favor down on me today.

WHEN WRONGS
ARE MADE RIGHT

*"How long, O Lord, holy and true, will
You not judge and avenge our blood
on those who dwell on the earth?"*

REVELATION 6:10

This prayer is enough to send chills down the spine of anyone who reads it. The speakers: "the souls of those who were slain for the word of God" (verse 9). The setting: an altar before the throne of God in heaven.

The picture it paints is as poignant as it is unsettling: a multitude of billions, seated just behind the thin veil that separates this life from the eternal hereafter, locked in an anguished plea for justice to be performed on the earth they once called home—a plea that echoes our own feeble cries as we walk the earth today.

When evil seems to prevail and justice seems to hide its face—when we're consumed by questions and doubts and fears that maybe our lives and efforts are all in vain—we must remember the response God gives to these despairing cries: *Peace, my children. Rest now, for soon, all will be made right* (Revelation 6:11). Before long, as the rest of the book of Revelation shows, God *will* step in and make His glory known. He *will* reward His children for the suffering they've endured. And He *will* dispense justice on all those who dared fight against His chosen.

But until then, we wait patiently with the prayers of the martyrs on our lips. A new heaven and a new earth are coming (21:1), and its glory will be worth the pain.

FOR FURTHER THOUGHT:

- When was the last time you were hurt by injustice?
- How might the fact that the saints in heaven feel the same way give you the strength to press on?

PRAYER STARTER:

Lord, my prayer is to see Your righteousness displayed on the earth. I long for the day when all wrongs are made right.

UNWORTHY

We acknowledge, O LORD, our wickedness and the iniquity of our fathers, for we have sinned against You. Do not hate us, for Your name's sake; do not disgrace the throne of Your glory. Remember, do not break Your covenant with us.
JEREMIAH 14:20–21

Jeremiah had no delusions about his nation's standing with God. He knew his people had collectively blown it. There was no reason for God not to wipe them from the face of the earth. Well, no reason except one: God's everlasting covenant.

Throughout Israel's history, God had promised to preserve at least a remnant of His people, to show mercy on a nation that didn't deserve even a shred of His grace. So Jeremiah came before God on behalf of a people with zero credentials—not a single righteous deed to show for—and begged for His favor.

As Christians who are saved by nothing but Jesus' sacrificial blood, we understand Jeremiah's plea. Each day, we fall before God with nothing to show for it but the grace that was gained for us on the cross. We beg for His favor on our lives—for forgiveness, blessings, and guidance—even though we know we don't deserve it. And because of God's promises to forget our sin-stained past, to bury it beneath the cleansing flood of His mercy, He is always willing to listen to our humble prayers.

FOR FURTHER THOUGHT:

- What would it take for a man to earn God's favor on his own?
- Why did God even bother making a covenant with such unreliable people such as us?

PRAYER STARTER:

Father, please pour out Your blessings on my life. I know I'm not worthy on my own—it's only the blood of Jesus that makes me clean in Your eyes.

WHEN GOD HIDES

Why do You stand afar off, O Lᴏʀᴅ? Why do You hide Yourself in times of trouble?. . . Arise, O Lᴏʀᴅ. O God, lift up Your hand; do not forget the humble.
Psᴀʟᴍ 10:1, 12

It's a question as old as time: Why does God—the Creator of the cosmos; the lover of our souls—seem to always be hiding from His creation? Sure, He's made His existence clear throughout our amazing universe, but why doesn't He just step in and make Himself fully known from time to time? Why does He let evil run rampant while His children cry out? When we stare at the sky in frustration, why can't we see His face?

In this life, we may never be able to fully answer these questions. God is a God of mysteries. After all, if we knew everything about Him, He wouldn't be God—He'd be a product of our own imagination. The human mind just isn't strong enough to grasp the infinite—to understand the complex motives that drive God's silence.

But as today's psalm proves, God still wants us to ask. He's still willing to grant His favor to those who humble themselves before Him, broken and confused.

Even if we never get the answer we're looking for, God can still lift up His hand and comfort us through our tears, assuring His children that we're never truly alone.

FOR FURTHER THOUGHT:

- How did God "break His silence" when He sent Jesus?
- How is God with believers in His perceived silence?

PRAYER STARTER:

Father God, I know I'll never know everything about You on this side of eternity. But today, please rise up and remember me, Lord. Remind me that You're still here, even in the silence.

PRAYERS OF THANKSGIVING AND PRAISE

PRACTICE RUN

"Blessing and honor and glory and power be to Him who sits on the throne and to the Lamb forever and ever."
REVELATION 5:13

When we Christian men think of prayer, the first thing that comes to mind is often some kind of request. And while God certainly expects us to ask Him for our hearts' deepest needs and desires, today's verse shows what kind of prayer we'll be praying in heaven for all eternity: prayers of thanksgiving and praise.

Since heaven will be perfect, there will be no need to ask God for anything. Everything we'll need will be right there in front of us, shining in all His glory forever. But while we're on this earth, we get tiny glimpses of this higher reality—blessings, small and large, that counterbalance the crushing sorrow and pain we feel from time to time. And because these blessings foreshadow our eternal existence with God, our response to these blessings should follow suit. After all, how strange would it be to not enjoy the act of thanking God. . .when that's exactly what you're looking forward to doing for all eternity? Our tiny expressions of thankfulness here are just practice runs for our eternal gratitude that will one day flood our souls.

So today, take some time to thank the one who makes this eternal life possible.

FOR FURTHER THOUGHT:

- How does the prospect of thanking God for eternity give us yet another reason to praise Him?

- In what ways are you living this life in preparation for the one to come?

PRAYER STARTER:

Even if I praised You every second for the rest of my life, God, I know it still wouldn't be enough. I'd need an eternity, which is exactly what You offer. Thank You for this breathtaking promise.

PRIORITIES

"Our Father who is in heaven, hallowed be
Your name. Your kingdom come. Your will
be done on earth as it is in heaven."
MATTHEW 6:9–10

When it comes to prayer, what's your highest priority? Making sure God hears you and gives you what you want, or bringing the maximum amount of glory to His name? Today's passage, which contains the first part of Jesus' model prayer, tells us where Jesus' priorities truly lay.

Of all the ways Jesus could have begun His prayer, He chose praise and humility. By recognizing God's holiness and sovereignty at the start, Jesus put the rest of the prayer in its proper context. We don't pray for food, forgiveness, and deliverance from sin because we have our own ideas of what's best for us; we pray for these things to be done in accordance with God's will. God isn't a magic genie that grants wishes. He's the source of our very existence. All we can do is acknowledge His power and humbly pray that our life aligns with His plan.

Today, when you fall before God in prayer—whether

it's for something as huge as a career change or as small as a backache—begin your request by lifting up His name and thanking Him for what He's already done. That way, once the proper context is set, the rest of your prayer will fall firmly within His will.

FOR FURTHER THOUGHT:

- Why do you think Jesus not only began His prayer with praise but ended it that way as well (Matthew 6:13)?

- What does the structure of your daily prayers look like?

PRAYER STARTER:

Lord God, I praise You for Your power and unfathomable glory. Please let my life align with Your master plan, God. Thank You for always knowing what's best.

SECOND CHANCES

I went down to the bottoms of the mountains;
the earth with her bars was around me
forever. Yet You have brought up my life
from corruption, O Lord my God.

JONAH 2:6

If anyone knew the relief that comes with a second chance, it was Jonah. Having foolishly fled from God in order to escape his responsibilities, Jonah found himself being swallowed by a gigantic fish. Surely, this was the end of the road for this wayward prophet. He was finally getting his just deserts.

But God saw the situation differently. Miraculously, Jonah lived through the experience, and he woke up in the fish's cavernous stomach. The place reeked of death, but Jonah knew that because he was still alive, God wasn't finished with him yet. So in what was perhaps the strangest setting for a "thank you," Jonah prayed the words of today's verse.

If you are a Christian, you know just how amazing God's second chances are. Not only have you been pulled from sin's watery grave, but you've also been clothed with the royal robes of righteousness and adopted into the family of God Himself. This didn't happen because of how good you were—just the opposite, in fact. God saved you despite the sins that plagued your past. When you ran from Him, He chased you until He found you, all because of the unfathomable love He has for the humans He's created.

Today, take some time to thank God for bringing your life up from corruption.

FOR FURTHER THOUGHT:

- Other than salvation, when did God last deliver you from danger?

- In what ways have you thanked Him for such mercies?

PRAYER STARTER:

*God, I don't understand the unending love
You have for me, and I certainly don't deserve it.
All I can do is thank You for giving me new life.*

CREATOR OF THE COSMOS

"You are worthy, O Lord, to receive glory and honor and power, for You have created all things, and for Your pleasure they are and were created."
REVELATION 4:11

Have you ever truly stopped to think how powerful God really is? You know God is mighty, of course—you read it in the Bible, hear it in sermons, and sing about it each Sunday. But have you ever considered the extent of His power?

Today's verse is an invitation to dwell on the unspeakable majesty of God.

Picture the world you know—your house, your neighborhood, your nation. And then zoom out until the entire world comes into view. . .and then keep zooming. Pretty soon, other planets start appearing, followed by a huge, blazing inferno we call the sun. Eventually, even this star becomes lost in a sea of light as thousands, then millions, then billions of stars combine to form our galaxy. . .which then gets lost in a milky blend of trillions of galaxies, all shimmering like candles in a vast, black, expanding cosmos.

Now travel back in time and imagine the creation

of this cosmos. With a single word, the author of existence, throned in His timeless, eternal realm, brought everything into being without lifting a finger. He stretched out the heavens like a tent, peppering it with light and stardust. And why? For *His pleasure*. The air we breathe, the world we inhabit, the space through which our feeble planet hurdles—all was created as a stage for His glory to be displayed.

Today, dwell on the God who surpasses imagination, and praise Him for His awesome glory.

FOR FURTHER THOUGHT:

- When did you last stop to think about how powerful God is?
- Why do you think such an amazing being invites us to dwell on His majesty?

PRAYER STARTER:

Lord God, You are incredible. Confronted with Your splendor, I can do nothing but fall down and worship You as King.

THANKFUL TO SERVE

"Both riches and honor come from You, and You reign over all. And in Your hand is power and might, and in Your hand it is to make great and to give strength to all. Now therefore, our God, we thank You and praise Your glorious name."
1 Chronicles 29:12–13

This prayer comes on the heels of one of Israel's most defining moments—the beginning of the construction of God's temple. As the people volunteered assistance with "perfect heart" (1 Chronicles 29:9), David was overwhelmed with a bubbling sense of joy. For years, he'd dreamed of this moment, and now to see it come to pass before his very eyes was almost too much for him to take in. All he could do was offer up this heartfelt prayer of thanksgiving to God for allowing His name to be glorified through Solomon, David's son.

How often do you praise God for the ability to shine His light on others? You've been gifted with the most important, most glorious kingdom in existence, and the King has given you the responsibility to share it with others. How amazing is that? Each moment of your life—each decision you make to live in God's will—is a chance to place one more stone into the temple of your life for God's glory.

Today, come to God as His grateful son. With thanksgiving in your heart, praise Him for gifting His heavenly treasures to men.

FOR FURTHER THOUGHT:

- Why is it sometimes tempting to view God's command to share the gospel as an obligation and not a gift?
- How can a Christian man replace this attitude with thankfulness?

PRAYER STARTER:

Thank You, Father, for the chance to lift up Your name. May I never miss an opportunity to bring glory to You.

BIG UNIVERSE; BIGGER LOVE

When I consider Your heavens, the work of Your fingers, the moon and the stars, which You have ordained, what is man that You are mindful of him? And the son of man that You care about him?

PSALM 8:3–4

One great way to consider your relationship with God is to look at the scale of His creation, the scale of your existence, and the scale of His love toward you.

The size of this universe—this sprawling, stretching expanse that we call reality—dwarfs our deepest hopes and fears by comparison. Human logic would tell us, "Who cares about whether one guy can pay his bills or feed his family? He's just a speck walking on a slightly bigger speck in the middle of a sea of exploding stars and colliding galaxies." It's really hard to see how the Creator of such a vast domain could care about one of His tiniest creations on a little blue marble called Earth.

But thankfully, God cares anyway.

And this doesn't mean He just shows a passing concern. No, He's committed to our well-being—so committed, in fact, that He went through the trouble to come down, live among us, and die on our behalf. If only one person existed, that person would hold infinitely more value in God's eyes than a trillion universes stacked together. We are more than stardust—we are living souls, made in the image of the one who gave us life.

Today, let's praise Him for His incredible love.

FOR FURTHER THOUGHT:

- How committed is God to your well-being?
- Why do you think God made such a huge universe, knowing all we'd need is one small planet?

PRAYER STARTER:

Almighty Father, I can't fathom the love You have toward me—or even why You would love me at all. All I can do is pour out my gratitude today.

GOD'S RIGHTEOUS JUDGMENTS

"Salvation and glory and honor and power to the Lord our God. For His judgments are true and righteous."
REVELATION 19:1–2

We've all felt the heat of God's discipline at one time or another. Having slipped into a pattern of unwise behavior, we suddenly feel overwhelmed with conviction as we see our circumstances heading south and our souls running dry for lack of God's blessing.

So what's our response when we find ourselves on the wrong side of God's righteousness? To become bitter and resentful toward the paradigm of holiness? Or to recognize God's goodness and humbly submit to His correction?

Today's verse invites us to thank God for his true and righteous judgments. Of course, this can be hard for a man who's wrong but earnestly thinks he's right. To him, God's correction comes across as an annoyance—an obstacle to be overcome while he selfishly pursues his vision of the way his life should be. But to a man of God, the Lord's judgments come as a relief—a welcome road sign guiding him back to the path from which he's strayed. He knows there's no point in resisting God's discipline. It's not even an option. The only thing left to do is to praise God for once again showing His grace by extending a second chance.

Which kind of man are you?

FOR FURTHER THOUGHT:

- Why do you think God disciplines His children?

- What would the world be like if there were no consequences for sin?

PRAYER STARTER:

Father God, I'll be honest—I don't like it when I'm being disciplined. But looking back, I'm able to see the good changes Your correction has brought about in me. Thank You for Your righteous judgments.

IGNORE THE HATERS

And when the chief priests and scribes saw the wonderful things that He did, and the children crying in the temple and saying, "Hosanna to the Son of David," they were greatly displeased.
MATTHEW 21:15

Today's verse is almost humorous in the way it juxtaposes the people's praise with the religious leaders' contempt. The crowd's proclamations were like a freely gushing fountain that the scribes were scrambling desperately to plug. Having seen Jesus' miracles, these leaders must have known in their hearts that His message was true, but they didn't care—their own popularity had to be preserved at all costs.

Well, the crowd didn't care either. More specifically, they didn't care if these leaders were happy or not—they were too busy praising the Messiah, whom they'd been expecting for centuries. It was going to take a lot more than a few stuffy men in elaborate robes to stop them from praising the long-awaited Son of God as He passed by.

Are we Christian men that enthusiastic about God's love? When the world tells us to "stop being so fanatical," do we lower our gaze and shamefully comply? Or do our voices get louder, drowning out the naysayers? When the Christian life gets rough and we feel like we're the only ones serving God, the act of praise is the one thing that can elevate us above the static and give strength to our bones.

Today, choose to ignore the haters. . .and focus on God's perfect love instead.

FOR FURTHER THOUGHT:

- What would the world be like if Christians caved into every pressure the world exerted on them?

- How would the gospel grow if Christian men kept it silent?

PRAYER STARTER:

Thank You, Father, for Your matchless grace and Your undying love! I don't care if people think I'm strange for this gratitude—all I care about is pleasing You.

PULLED FROM THE GRAVE

Therefore my heart is glad, and my glory rejoices. My flesh also shall rest in hope. For You will not leave my soul in hell, nor will You allow Your Holy One to see corruption.

PSALM 16:9–10

One of the best things about the book of Psalms is the multiple layers that lay within each prayer. Today's passage, for example, was prayed by David as he praised God for preserving his life from his enemies. But it's also a poignant description of Jesus' death, burial, and resurrection—an acknowledgment of the fact that God's Son would not stay dead in the grave but would instead rise victoriously. And because of Jesus' resurrection, this passage is also a description of every Christian's relationship with God.

Before you accepted Jesus, you were a sinner, destined for the fires of God's righteous wrath. But the moment you pled for forgiveness and turned from your sin, God reached down to your muddy pit, scooped you up in His mighty hand, and placed you in a castle of gold. And when you finally breathe your last, your destination lies not in the pit of judgment but in the eternal peace of God's protection. Your soul will not see corruption—instead, it will shine like the sun forever.

How often do you thank God for conducting such an amazing rescue mission—for ensuring that His children will have only the best for all eternity? Today, fall before His feet and praise Him for pulling you from your spiritual grave.

FOR FURTHER THOUGHT:

- Would you say you are more focused on your trials or eternity?

- How can you begin to focus even more on eternity, where all corruption in your heart will be erased?

PRAYER STARTER:

Thank You, God, for saving me from such an awful fate. Because of Your grace, I no longer fear the grave— it's just the final stepping stone in my journey home.

SAYING GRACE

And when He had taken the five loaves and the two fish, He looked up to heaven, and blessed and broke the loaves, and gave them to His disciples to set before them, and He divided the two fish among them all.

MARK 6:41

Those who grew up in Christian homes were probably taught the importance of "saying grace" before a meal. Maybe the act of bowing your head before digging in has become such an important part of your life that it's almost second nature to you. You may not even think about it—the words just escape your lips in a silent stream of routine recitation before you open your eyes and pick up the fork.

Today's verse says that Jesus blessed His food too. But if there's one thing we know about Jesus, nothing He ever did in relation to prayer was "mindless" or "routine." He was intentional in His relationship with God. . .even when it came to common, everyday activities.

By praying over your food each day and taking the time to dwell on the words, thanksgiving will gradually become an inseparable part of your life. You don't have to wax eloquent or start pontificating on the finer points of theology—just a simple, heartfelt "Thank You, God, for providing yet another meal" is enough to begin developing an attitude of gratitude.

FOR FURTHER THOUGHT:

- How many of your prayers would you say are routine?

- How might you start revitalizing those routines today?

PRAYER STARTER:

Father God, I know all good things come from You— and that includes this meal. Thank You, God, for this food, as well as for all the tiny blessings in my life.

TURN BACK

And one of them, when he saw that he was healed,
turned back, and with a loud voice glorified
God, and fell down on his face at His feet,
giving Him thanks. And he was a Samaritan.
LUKE 17:15–16

Out of the ten lepers who were healed that day, only one understood that prayer is a two-step process. All ten knew Jesus could heal them, so they had no problem taking the first step: the request. But when Jesus answered them, all but one forgot about the second step: thanksgiving.

While we don't know the exact contents of this lone former leper's prayer, today's passage says it involved "a loud voice" and him falling "on his face at [Jesus'] feet." This man—who for years had known nothing but shame and a gradual deterioration of health—wasn't about to just go on with his life in the same manner. His heart overflowed with gratitude, and the only way he knew how to express it was by falling at his Savior's feet.

How easy it is for a Christian man to pray for God to meet a need. . .but how hard it is sometimes for that same man to give thanks once that need is met. Often, we get so caught up in the excitement that we simply forget to say, "Thank You." But if left unchecked, this carelessness can cause us to forget the very source of our blessings, and we may even start bragging about ourselves.

Today, follow the Samaritan leper's example and—whenever God grants your request—turn back and give Him the thanks He deserves.

FOR FURTHER THOUGHT:

- How has God blessed you in ways you haven't thanked Him for?

- How can you make sure no answered prayers "slip through the cracks" of your "thank You" list?

PRAYER STARTER:

Lord, I want to be like the Samaritan leper.
May gratitude be my natural reaction
whenever I encounter Your blessings.

GOD'S "GREATEST HITS"

"You have made heaven, the heaven of heavens,
with all their host, the earth and all things that
are in it. . . . You are the LORD God, who chose
Abram and brought him forth out of Ur of the
Chaldeans. . . . And You saw the affliction of our
fathers in Egypt, and heard their cry by the Red Sea."
NEHEMIAH 9:6–7, 9

As the Israelites stood at the edge of a new chapter in their nation's history, it must have been hard for them to put their gratitude into words. What single prayer could possibly encompass the depth of the blessings God had shown them by allowing Jerusalem to be restored? Such a feat was impossible. . .but the Israelites were willing to try.

To begin the longest recorded prayer in scripture, the Israelites launched into a description of God's "greatest hits," realizing this day would forever be engraved on that list. By remembering the past—the mountains and valleys through which God had led this fledgling nation—the Israelites looked with eager anticipation toward the future.

Looking back through your life, what are some of

God's "greatest hits"—important milestones in your walk with Him? Maybe the list begins with your salvation at a young age and spans decades of spiritual blessings. Or maybe you're a relatively new convert, and your list includes the myriad choices and events that, in hindsight, were leading you toward His grace.

Either way, it's never too early or late to start praising God for the story He's writing in your life.

FOR FURTHER THOUGHT:

- Other than your salvation, what is one of God's greatest hits in your spiritual journey?

- How often do you thank God for past blessings, not just the ones that are happening now?

PRAYER STARTER:

Author of life, You've been writing my story all this time. Thank You for each chapter of blessings that I've lived so far—and all the chapters coming in the future.

REJOICE!

My heart rejoices in the LORD; my horn is exalted in the LORD. My mouth is enlarged over my enemies, because I rejoice in Your salvation.
1 SAMUEL 2:1

Hannah knew what it's like to "wait on the LORD" (Psalm 27:14). For years, she'd fallen before God in tears, begging Him for a child. . .and for years, God had seemingly remained silent in the presence of such pain and longing. So when God finally answered her prayer and gave her Samuel, there was nothing Hannah could do but rejoice and thank the one who had shown her the favor.

Hannah's response sets a perfect example for believers today. Often, the amount of time we spend thanking God pales in comparison to the time and energy we spend asking Him to act. We pray for long periods, begging God to meet a need. But then when He finally does answer, we offer up a quick "thank You" (if we're feeling generous) and go on our way. Hannah, however, knew better than to take God's mercy for granted. So, in one of the most moving prayers in the Bible, she launched into a lengthy session of gratitude, praising God for His kindness and glory.

As Christians, we've been given the ultimate proof of God's love: deliverance from sin. In the face of such an infinite gift, how could we not fall to our knees each day and proclaim, "I rejoice in Your salvation"?

FOR FURTHER THOUGHT:

- Why do you think gratitude is sometimes a learned art rather than a natural response?

- How can you improve your gratitude today?

PRAYER STARTER:

Father God, I know I'll never be able to thank You enough for Your love. . .but that won't stop me from trying. I praise You today for Your great grace.

GOD'S BEEN GOOD

"Naked I came out of my mother's womb and naked I shall return there. The LORD gave and the LORD has taken away. Blessed be the name of the LORD."

JOB 1:21

Few people have had it rougher than Job. Not only were his family, possessions, and health brutally stolen from him, but the two sources of comfort he had left—his wife and three friends—were either telling him to curse God or wrongly accusing him of sin. His pain must have been unfathomable; his confusion, justified.

So what was Job's first reaction to so cruel a fate? Did he lash out at God, following his wife's suggestion and forfeiting his life? Did he wallow in pity, telling God, "There must be some mistake"? No. Instead, Job praised God, his Creator.

When he could not find anything in his life for which he could be thankful, he thanked God for God's own unchanging nature. Job knew that as long as God was still God, he could find refuge in the goodness and righteousness of the Lord. Everything that happened to him had to have a purpose, and that purpose would one day be revealed.

What a profound example for Christian men today. When tragedy strikes, it's tempting to throw a pity party and give God the cold shoulder. But as Job's prayer shows—and as the end of his story later reveals—God is never undeserving of our praise, even when all evidence seems to say otherwise. In the end, we will stand with Job in the heavenly kingdom, looking back at our life with the knowledge that God has *always* been good.

FOR FURTHER THOUGHT:

- When have you been tempted to doubt God's character?
- How might Job's prayer offer you a new perspective on His goodness?

PRAYER STARTER:

Thank You, Lord Jesus, for life—for the joys as well as the pain. I know Your purposes are higher than mine, so I humbly praise You today.

CONSTANT GRATITUDE

Now when Daniel knew that the writing was signed, he went to his house, and—his windows being open in his room toward Jerusalem—he knelt on his knees three times a day and prayed and gave thanks before his God, as he did formerly.

DANIEL 6:10

If you went to God in prayer one day knowing this act would ensure your death at the hands of your enemies, what would your prayer consist of? Would it be a complaint? A cry for help? A plea for God to judge those who persecute you?

Well, that's exactly the situation Daniel found himself in. And out of all the prayers he could have prayed, the Bible says he "gave thanks before his God, as he did formerly."

To Daniel, gratitude was more than an optional step he took after God granted his request. It was his lifeblood—his best way of connecting with the God who spiritually sustained him in his pagan culture. If thanking God would result in his demise, then so be it—he would die with a song of praise on his lips.

Do you value thanksgiving as much as Daniel did?

171

When you kneel before God each day, do you make sure to thank Him for the miracles—big and small—He has wrought in your life? As Daniel's story shows, gratitude is so much more than a couple of words said in relief after a brush with disaster—it's a lifestyle of continuous praise toward the one who gives us our breath. After all, it's never possible to thank Him too much.

FOR FURTHER THOUGHT:

- Why do you think God values our prayers of gratitude so much?

- How does thanksgiving strengthen us in our walk with Him?

PRAYER STARTER:

Lord God, I want to thank You for everything—my life, health, family, friends, home, blessings, and salvation. Help me to never forget to be grateful.

PRAYERS OF
INTERCESSION

A CHANCE FOR REDEMPTION

> *"Will You also destroy the*
> *righteous with the wicked?"*
> GENESIS 18:23

Through their persistent, gross violations of God's laws, the cities of Sodom and Gomorrah had long tested God's patience. Soon, their overdue punishment would finally arrive—there would be no survivors.

When God told Abraham this sobering truth, what was his response? Was he thrilled at the prospect of God's wrath being poured out on these evil cities? Or was he apathetic, shrugging it off with a mere "good thing it's not my problem"?

Neither. Instead, Abraham was horrified. "But Lord," he exclaimed, "what if there are good people living there? Maybe the city still has a chance! Surely, You'd spare the city for a few righteous souls. Right, God?" Abraham wasn't making excuses for Sodom and Gomorrah's sin—he knew they deserved punishment. Instead, his heart was so attuned with God's that his soul ached over the thought of premature judgment. As long as there were righteous people in the city (which, sadly, we later learn that there were not), he knew there was a chance for redemption.

As our culture drifts further from God, it's easy for a Christian man to feel angry and impatient with God for allowing this. . .or to simply bar himself from the world and pretend everything is okay. But as Abraham's story shows, neither response honors God. It's time for Christian men to step up to the front lines, praying on behalf of our neighbors and friends. Who knows? There may still be time for repentance.

FOR FURTHER THOUGHT:

- Have you ever known someone you thought was beyond repentance. . .but who later proved you wrong by accepting Christ?

- How might that person's example illustrate the importance of Abraham's prayer?

PRAYER STARTER:

God, I know there are still righteous people in my wayward culture. So, if possible, please extend Your mercy as You continue working to draw all men to You.

IN-HOUSE PRAYING

*[I] do not cease to give thanks for you,
making mention of you in my prayers, that
the God of our Lord Jesus Christ, the Father
of glory, may give to you the spirit of wisdom
and revelation in the knowledge of Him.*

EPHESIANS 1:16–17

It's great to pray for wisdom and spiritual growth for yourself—in fact, the Bible repeatedly encourages it. But what about praying for these things to be found in others?

In verse 15, Paul says he had "heard of [the Ephesians Christians'] faith in the Lord Jesus and love for all the saints." And once he'd found out about this community of spiritually thriving believers, he was immediately prompted to thank God and pray for their spiritual well-being.

Whenever we hear of someone coming to Christ, it's tempting to just stop at the first part of Paul's prayer—thanksgiving. But as today's passage shows, there's so much more to the Christian life than taking the first step. It's a lifelong journey, filled with ups and downs and blessings and loss. We all need others to pray for us as we press onward toward our goal.

How often do you pray for the Christians in your community. . .in your nation. . .in your world? Are you attentive to the "spiritual climate" around you, always looking for new opportunities to expand your prayer list? Or are you content with just minding your own business?

Today, take some time to offer a quick prayer for a newfound child of God. After all, that person is now part of your family.

FOR FURTHER THOUGHT:

- As a Christian, when have you desperately needed someone to pray for you?
- How might you offer that help to someone today?

PRAYER STARTER:

Father, I know there are so many brothers and sisters in Christ who need prayer. Make me aware of their needs and remind me to pray for their spiritual growth.

WHEN LEADERS FAIL

*O Lord, to us belongs confusion of face, to our
kings, to our princes, and to our fathers, because
we have sinned against You. . . . O my God,
incline Your ear and hear. Open Your eyes
and behold our desolations and the city that is
called by Your name. For we do not present our
supplications before You because of our righteous
acts, but because of Your great mercies.*
DANIEL 9:8, 18

If anyone knew how severe the consequences were for
bad leadership, it was Daniel. He'd seen his own nation
fall due to corrupt leaders, he'd watched as God literally spelled out judgments upon the Babylonian ruler
Belshazzar, and he'd listened in awe as angels foretold
the downfall of mighty kings. Daniel understood that in
order for a kingdom to thrive, its leaders had to follow
God's commands.

How scary is it to apply this truth to modern times? It
seems that precious few leaders obey or even recognize
God's laws. And even the ones who do are often soon
corrupted by the lure of fame and popularity.

So today, take time to pray for your country and

179

your leaders. Pray that they will wake up to the truth found in God's Word. God isn't willing that any should perish (2 Peter 3:9), so pray that He will have mercy on a nation that's gone astray—that He'll grant them more time to turn to Him.

Today, be a man who stands on behalf of his people. Be bold enough to ask for the impossible. Be a Daniel.

FOR FURTHER THOUGHT:

- When you hear of laws and policies you don't agree with, what's your first reaction: anger or prayer?
- Which leaders can you pray for today?

PRAYER STARTER:

Thank You, Father, for Your unending mercy. My nation needs some of that mercy today, God. Please teach us all how to walk in the light of Your commands.

IMPROBABLE MERCY

*"Father, forgive them, for they do
not know what they do."*

LUKE 23:34

In a very real sense, Jesus' prayer in today's verse was more accurate than anyone present could have guessed. Even though the Roman soldiers were guilty of murder, they had no way of knowing that the Man they were murdering was truly the Son of God. Their sin went beyond its already-awful boundaries and stepped into a territory that no mortal had yet explored—violence against the Divine.

Think of the last time someone said something unthinkably cruel to you—something that still echoes in your mind long after the dust has settled. Chances are, you first felt shocked by that person's audacity. Then the shock turned to anger. . .then to depression. . .and then to a deep-seated resentment. You may still harbor feelings of ill will toward that individual, secretly waiting for a day of reckoning for those awful words.

But Jesus' prayer on the cross flips everything we know about bitterness and anger on its head. Instead of focusing on the sin that these Romans *knew* they were committing, Jesus focused on the innocence caused by what they *didn't* know. Instead of wishing for a day of reckoning, Jesus sincerely wanted God to have mercy on them.

What a powerful expression of God's love. Even in the throes of death brought about by mankind's wicked arrogance, Jesus searched for a glimmer of redemption for their souls.

Are you willing to pray for your enemies today?

FOR FURTHER THOUGHT:

- When has someone shown mercy toward you after you wronged that person?
- How did that act of love impact your life?

PRAYER STARTER:

God, I've been hurt by careless words many times, but I realize that many of these comments probably stemmed from a lack of understanding. Forgive them for this, and help me move on.

SIBLING RIVALRY

"Heal her now, O God, I beseech You."
NUMBERS 12:13

Today's prayer comes near the end of a particularly ugly story about a sibling dispute. Miriam and Aaron, Moses' sister and brother, had just finished complaining about Moses' marriage to an Ethiopian woman—a complaint that actually stemmed from their jealousy over his popularity (verse 2). Moses, being extraordinarily meek (verse 3), apparently said nothing in response. . .until God Himself took up for him by striking Miriam with leprosy.

What was Moses' reaction? Did he use the sudden punishment as an opportunity to gloat? Did he reprimand her for her bad behavior? No. Instead, Moses *prayed* for her.

Obviously, the fact that Miriam was Moses' sister must have factored into his concerned plea. As much as his siblings had pestered him and tarnished his reputation, he still loved them as only a brother could. So he definitely didn't want to see one of them struck with a horrible disease on his behalf.

How do you react when other Christians seem to

stab you in the back? Being hurt by an ungodly scoffer is painful enough—but sibling betrayal is the ultimate insult. It's tempting to rejoice whenever these people get their just desserts. But in order for the body of Christ to flourish, forgiveness must flourish as well. So when you see a brother or sister fall, don't hesitate to put the past behind you and ask God to pick that person back up again.

It's just what siblings do.

FOR FURTHER THOUGHT:

- What is your first instinct or reaction when a fellow believer betrays you?
- How can you ensure that you react more like Moses in the future?

PRAYER STARTER:

Lord, show me how to pray for my brothers and sisters in Christ—even the ones who've done me wrong. I don't want any of them to stumble in their walk with You.

BATTLE LINES

*Brothers, my heart's desire and prayer to
God for Israel is that they might be saved.*

ROMANS 10:1

Paul was used to living on the battleground between two
faiths. During his time as a Jew, he gained a frightening
reputation amongst the Christians as he mercilessly
tracked them down—all while, unbeknownst to him,
God tracked him down as well. But even after his con-
version, he stayed on the battle lines for quite some
time, focusing his efforts on reaching the very people
he'd once joined in persecuting Christians.

In short, there was no way for Paul to escape his
Jewish background. He loved his people deeply, and
even though he no longer shared their worldview, he
prayed each day for their salvation. He was a man of
his culture who sought to change it through prayer.

As a modern Christian man, you may feel disheart-
ened by the rapid changes you see in your culture.
Christian values which were once strongly held by many
are now receding further and further into unpopularity
or even disdain. So what's a man to do? Shut himself
off from the world and never speak to anyone except

on Sunday morning? Relax his morals and accept sin?

Neither! Instead, he should do as Paul did: *pray.* Pray for the redemption of the people in this culture. Intercede for them to God, begging Him to pierce the growing darkness with His light. When enough Christian men stand their ground by falling to their knees, that's when true and lasting change will begin.

FOR FURTHER THOUGHT:

- What areas of culture do you most want to see changed?

- How can you start praying for this today?

PRAYER STARTER:

Lord, my prayer is that my entire nation will be saved. Start bringing about that revival today.

"IT'S ALL MY FAULT"

"Behold, I have sinned, and I have done wickedly. But these sheep, what have they done? Let Your hand, I ask, be against me and against my father's house."

2 SAMUEL 24:17

King David had messed up. Again. Against his better judgment—and against God's voice that spoke within his heart and through the mouth of Joab, his commander—David took a census of his people. Why this was sinful, we can only guess. Perhaps it had something to do with the pride in David's heart at the time, or maybe it was simply because God had forbidden it. Either way, David knew what he was about to do was wrong. . .and he did it anyway.

God, naturally, wasn't pleased, so He sent an angel to strike the people with a fatal plague. David, upon seeing the tens of thousands who had already died, cried out the words in today's prayer. Because David was, at his core, a righteous king who loved his people, he didn't want any of them to suffer as a result of his own careless behavior. Instead, he called on God to punish him instead.

Do we as Christian men love our neighbor like David did? Whenever we see a fellow human suffering, are we willing to step in and bear that person's pain ourselves? It takes a special kind of love to pray David's prayer—a love that would scarcely be seen again until the birth of Jesus Christ, our ultimate example.

FOR FURTHER THOUGHT:

- How does David's story disprove the popular expression, "I'm hurting no one except myself"?

- When have you willingly taken the punishment for a wrong you could have pushed off on someone else?

PRAYER STARTER:

Lord, I don't want anyone to suffer for the wrongs I've done. Give me the grace and love to accept the blame and punishment whenever it's due.

AN EYE-OPENING EXPERIENCE

"LORD, I ask, open his eyes that he may see."
2 KINGS 6:17

Things weren't looking good for Elisha and his servant. The Syrian army had surrounded the city of Dothan, where the prophet lived, and was ready to attack at any moment. Elisha's servant shook in his boots, probably thinking to himself, *I didn't sign up for this!*

Obviously, the servant knew all about Elisha's record—how God had worked miracles through him time and time again. But there's just something about the sight of a massive army closing in from all directions that makes people forget those details.

So, in order to cure his servant's temporary paralysis, Elisha asked God to give this man a different image to focus on—another army, much larger than the Syrians and consisting of horses and chariots of fire. This spiritual cavalry was more than enough to ease the servant's concerns. . .especially after he saw God's troops striking the Syrians with blindness.

Do you know someone who suffers from crippling fear? Maybe that person is an otherwise strong Christian who just can't handle some of the stresses that life brings. If so, follow Elisha's example and pray for this individual. Pray that God will open this Christian's eyes to the invisible army all around us, thus enabling that person to better focus on a closer walk with the Lord.

FOR FURTHER THOUGHT:

- When have you had an "eye-opening" experience in your walk with God?
- How might you use the memory of this experience to sincerely pray that God will give it to someone else?

PRAYER STARTER:

Lord God, thank You for opening the eyes of Your children whenever we are afraid. May I always be searching for an opportunity to pray for a fellow brother or sister's struggling faith.

A HEART FOR FAMILY

"I do not ask that You take them out of the world, but that You would keep them from evil. They are not of the world, even as I am not of the world. Sanctify them through Your truth. Your word is truth."

JOHN 17:15–17

Jesus' prayer in John 17 is one of the clearest glimpses we get of His heart for those who believe in Him. As He stood on the verge of an incomprehensibly painful death, the primary thought that surged through His mind was this: *Father, when I'm gone, take care of Your children.*

Are we that invested in the plight of our fellow believers? When we hear of people giving their lives to Jesus, do we fall to our knees in prayer—first in thanksgiving and then in concern for their spiritual well-being? When we hear reports of persecution overseas, are we quick to pray for the safety and endurance of our brothers and sisters in Christ? Do we regularly ask God to grow a fellow Christian's spiritual maturity as he struggles through a world that's bent on seeing him fail?

If not, then maybe it's time for Jesus' prayer to become our own. If Jesus is truly our model for love and compassion, then shouldn't we follow His prayer life as well?

Today, make a list of fellow believers and start thinking of their specific spiritual needs. Then take this list to God, asking Him to work powerfully in each of their lives. The church needs Christian men who are willing to lift up one another in prayer.

FOR FURTHER THOUGHT:

- Among Christians you know or have heard about, who is struggling in matters of faith?
- What's the best prayer you can pray for them now?

PRAYER STARTER:

Lord, may Your church grow in strength and spiritual effectiveness. May all of Your children—myself included—commit themselves to a closer walk with You.

VIOLENT TIMES

*Why do You show me iniquity and cause
me to behold grievance? For plundering
and violence are before me, and there are
those who raise up strife and contention.*

HABAKKUK 1:3

The headlines scream of another school shooting. . .another supermarket stabbing. . .another officer killed in the line of duty. Meanwhile, a man with an unknown name lies bleeding in an unmarked alleyway, a wordless prayer for mercy on his lips.

How often do we see such evils and turn our heads? How often do we look at the faces of the victimized innocents and force ourselves not to care? How often do we simply forget to pray?

As society plunges down an ever-darkening tunnel of wickedness and violence without cause, Habakkuk's prayer grows disturbingly more relatable. Each half-hour news segment consists almost entirely of "plundering and violence," yet our willingness to pray seems to shrink with each passing day. If Christians won't stand in the gap for a culture dripping with injustice, who will? If we refuse to kneel before God on behalf of the innocent, how foolish all our talk of love and compassion becomes. It's time not only to pray but to put legs on our prayers, working fervently to make a better future and trusting God to bless our efforts.

Today, be the light in your community. Pray for God to infuse men's hearts with love instead of hatred. . .and then go out and show them how powerful this love really is.

FOR FURTHER THOUGHT:

- What are some ways Christian men can work toward stopping the violence in their land?

- How often do your pray for peace in your nation?

PRAYER STARTER:

Father God, I'm sick of seeing cruelty and suffering all around me. Only Your love can make a difference, so help me do my part and show this love to everyone I meet.

IMPENDING DOOM

"Ah, Lᴏʀᴅ God! Will you destroy all the rest of Israel
in Your pouring out of Your fury on Jerusalem?"
Eᴢᴇᴋɪᴇʟ 9:8

The book of Ezekiel is frightening in its vivid depictions of God's wrath. At first glance, it seems as if the author is reveling in the details of the sinners' suffering—as if both God and the prophet are enjoying the process of retribution.

Ezekiel 33:11, however, disproves such a horrid notion: "I have no pleasure in the death of the wicked," God says, "but that the wicked turns from his way and lives." And in today's prayer, we find that even Ezekiel himself is taken aback by the intensity of God's righteous fury upon His wayward people. The issue wasn't the magnitude of God's judgment; it was the gross severity of Israel's sin.

When we read about the fierce judgment that awaits those who mock God and His Word, are we gleeful with anticipation—like the prophet Jonah, eagerly camping outside the city of Nineveh and waiting for the fire to fall? Or do we, like Ezekiel, feel an immense sense of urgency over their fate? After all, the only thing that can save these people is the gospel. . .and God has handed it over to us. Instead of kicking back and waiting for the bitter end, we should be spreading the good news even more fervently and praying that it does not fall on deaf ears.

Who knows? Maybe God is holding off His fury, waiting for us to deliver the message that will turn people's hearts to Him.

FOR FURTHER THOUGHT:

- How often do you pray for the salvation of your community?
- What steps are you taking to try to bring it about?

PRAYER STARTER:

God, please show mercy toward my neighbors and friends who don't know You. Give them time to repent, and give me the courage to share the gospel with them whenever possible.

PRAYERS FOR THE PREACHER

"Let the LORD, the God of the spirits of all flesh, set a man over the congregation, who may go out before them and who may go in before them, and who may lead them out and who may bring them in, that the congregation of the LORD may not be as sheep that have no shepherd."
NUMBERS 27:16–17

Out of all the prayers in this book, this one may appear to be the *least* relatable. After all, when is the last time you prayed for the successful leadership of a struggling nation that had been directly chosen by God?

But what happens if you consider this verse from the perspective of God's *church*? Suddenly, this prayer becomes much more familiar. Chances are, you've been in a church that, for whatever reason, was forced to change its pastor. Sometimes, the process is smooth; other times, it can cause deep divisions in the church and plant seeds of bitterness and resentment amongst the congregation. Just like most decisions in life, the right choice isn't always immediately obvious—it often takes a healthy dose of hindsight to make things clear.

That's why today's prayer is so important. By praying

for God to set the right man over the congregation—or to simply give wisdom to the current leader—you are praying for the congregation as a whole. Just as a flock of sheep depends entirely on the shepherd, a church rises and falls with its pastor.

God wants His church to succeed in carrying out His mission on earth. Do you?

FOR FURTHER THOUGHT:

- How do you pray for your pastor?
- What are some ways you can get more acquainted with your pastor so you can pray for him?

PRAYER STARTER:

Today, God, I'm asking that You guide my pastor so he can successfully guide Your church.

PRAYERS FOR STRENGTH

BAD DECISIONS

"O LORD God, remember me, I ask. And strengthen me, I ask, only this once, O God, that I may at once take vengeance on the Philistines for my two eyes."
JUDGES 16:28

Samson was the poster child for bad decisions. He had a quick temper, a weakness for women, and an ego that was somehow even larger than his strength. He made nearly every mistake in the book—including revealing the secret of his power to a woman who'd already tried to have him killed multiple times. This last mistake would cost him his life. . .but not before Samson uttered the prayer in today's verse.

His strength gone, his eyes blinded, and his shame compounded by the knowledge that all of this could have been prevented, Samson cried out to God one last time. And guess what? God *listened*. Samson may have died that day, but his final Spirit-powered act dealt a major blow to God's enemies and ensured his placement in the Bible's "Hall of Faith" (Hebrews 11).

Chances are, you haven't messed up quite as bad as Samson. But even if you have, let today's prayer be your guide into a closer walk with Your Maker. No matter what kind of spiritual power you need—be it patience, the ability to love, or the strength to let go of the past—God is eager to grant it upon request. If you've truly repented, your past sins are dead and gone, buried under the infinite weight of God's grace. Each day is a new chance to step out and triumph over the enemy of your soul.

FOR FURTHER THOUGHT:

- Why do you think God often chooses to work through people (such as Samson, Paul, or Moses) who seem the most unqualified?

- How can today's prayer be your guide into a closer walk with God?

PRAYER STARTER:

*Thank You, God, for putting the past behind You.
I need Your power to flow through me today so I can
step into the brighter future You've planned for me.*

PERSONAL PEP TALK

I will love You, O LORD, my strength. The LORD
is my rock and my fortress and my deliverer.
PSALM 18:1–2

First Samuel 30 describes a distressing time for David. The city of Ziklag, where David's two wives lived, had been taken into captivity by the Amalekites. Such an overwhelming loss would be enough to put the strongest of men at his wit's end, but verse 6 reports how David responded: "[He] encouraged himself in the LORD his God."

What did that encouragement consist of? Well, given that David also wrote Psalm 18, his personal pep talk probably sounded a lot like today's prayer. God had delivered him through so much already—wild animals trying to kill his sheep, a giant with an outlandishly large sword and spear, and a mad king bent on taking his life. So what better way for David to encourage himself about the future than to look to his past? For David, God wasn't just a nice friend to have around or a neatly engraved Bible verse on his shepherd's staff; He was *everything* to him. Without God, there wasn't a chance David would even be alive.

Maybe you haven't fought giants or dodged spears, but if you're a Christian, you have at least one miracle you can point to as proof of God's presence: your deliverance from sin. When God saved you, He planted the seeds of strength in your spiritual bones. By remembering God's favor for you in the past, you can tap into this endless well of strength and bravely face whatever comes next.

FOR FURTHER THOUGHT:

- How often do you dwell on the ways God has saved you?

- How can remembering this give you strength and courage to face the future?

PRAYER STARTER:

Father God, You've brought me through so much already. I know this problem up ahead will be no different. Thank You.

SOUL-MELTING WEIGHT

My soul melts for heaviness.
Strengthen me according to Your word.
PSALM 119:28

The author of today's prayer had a way with words.

"My soul melts for heaviness," he wrote, conjuring images of a massive object crushing, grinding, and liquifying anything under its weight. What this weight was, we can only guess. If the author was David, as many believe, it might have been the death of his child after his grievous sin with Bathsheba. Or maybe it was the mental pressure of being hounded by a bloodthirsty King Saul. Or maybe it was just the overwhelming, day-to-day responsibilities he dealt with as a king.

Whatever the specific reason behind this heartfelt cry, its message is universal: we need God's strength. On our own, we're like ants attempting to carry the world. Not only can it not be done, it's foolish to even think of trying. It's enough to break one's spirit—to melt one's soul.

But thank God, we don't have to choose this depressing route. When heavy boulders of compacted grief and pain fall upon us, we can pray the second half of the psalmist's prayer: "Strengthen me according to Your word." The Bible is full of God's promises toward His children—peace, joy, hope, and an eternity of bliss with Him. So why try to bear the weight of the world alone? Ask God today to give you strength by reminding you of His unending love.

FOR FURTHER THOUGHT:

- How might the vagueness of today's prayer make it even more powerful?
- In what areas of your life can you apply its truth?

PRAYER STARTER:

Father God, I can't do this alone! I need You to strengthen my spiritual muscles so I can carry this massive weight.

A GUST FROM ABOVE

"And now, Lord, behold their threats and grant to Your servants that they may speak Your word with all boldness, by stretching out Your hand to heal, and that signs and wonders may be done by the name of Your holy child Jesus."

Acts 4:29–30

During Jesus' time on earth—and shortly after His ascension—His twelve disciples weren't exactly the dream team that many think they were. One of them had a quick temper and a tendency to not follow through on his promises, two of them were so belligerent that they were nicknamed "sons of thunder," one of them had been a greedy tax collector working for the Romans, one of them refused to believe in the resurrection at first, and all of them had a knack for arguing over who was the best of the bunch.

In short, they were human.

But now, these mere humans were charged with a task beyond the ability of any mortal—to take God's message to the ends of the earth. For that, they would need strength. A *lot* of strength. So, in today's verse, that's exactly what they prayed for.

No matter how bold you may be, you'll never be bold enough to fulfill God's calling using your power. You need help from above—a divine gust from the heavens that will empower you to spread His good news to all.

And all you need to do to obtain that power is pray.

FOR FURTHER THOUGHT:

- How long do you think the church would have lasted if God's power had not descended?

- Why do you think some Christian men try to go it alone?

PRAYER STARTER:

Heavenly Father, I need Your Spirit to convert my weakness to strength—to make me a bolder witness for Your grace. Please bestow that power upon me today.

THE GOD-MAGNET

Do not be far from me, for trouble is near, for there is no one to help.
PSALM 22:11

Too often, Christian men view God and tribulations like two south poles of a magnet, continually repelling each other. In other words, the closer trouble is to us, the farther God seems to be. The more we suffer, the more we think God has stepped back and left us on our own. As today's prayer shows, this is a very human reaction. . .but it also happens to be entirely wrong.

For the Christian man, in fact, the opposite is true. If a trial is the magnet's south pole, then God is its north. The closer trouble gets to our left side, the faster God rushes in to meet us at our right. So when you hit rock bottom, feeling as if there's no hope left, you can rest assured that God is right there with you, ready to lift you up. That's why, on almost every occasion, God's promises to be with His children come at a time when His children are in danger. Tribulation is a God-magnet, for only through pain can our relationship with Him grow stronger.

Do you feel like God is light-years away? Are you

struggling to find His presence in a sea of doubts and fear? Is the uncertainty of life finally taking a toll on your spirit? Rest assured: God is with You. And He'll continue to be with you until all trials pass into distant memory, overtaken by the steady pull of eternity.

FOR FURTHER THOUGHT:

- Why do you think God doesn't usually make His presence fully known when we want Him to?

- How did you end up feeling closer to God during your last tribulation?

PRAYER STARTER:

Lord God, I need strength for this battle. Remind me of Your unfailing presence through the midst of my pain.

UNQUALIFIED

And Moses said to the LORD, "O my Lord,
I am not eloquent, neither before now nor
since You have spoken to Your servant. But I
am slow of speech and of a slow tongue."
EXODUS 4:10

Isn't it strange how many Christian men treat their walk with God like a test of their own strength? Some pride themselves on being excellent orators, freely proclaiming the gospel with words as smooth as silk. Others boast of their own capacity for generosity, making sure to tell others in a roundabout way how much they gave last Sunday morning. Meanwhile, the same men might cower in a corner whenever God asks them to do something they're not comfortable with, afraid they'll never be strong enough to complete God's task.

Neither reaction is good. Instead, God wants us to look to Him as our source of strength. If we have strength in spades, we are to thank Him for giving it to us. If we are lacking, we are to step out nonetheless, trusting that God will fill in the gaps in our abilities.

That's the lesson Moses learned after today's prayer. He realized he was woefully incompetent, but he still stepped out in faith and obeyed God (admittedly, after more than a little prodding). Gradually, he learned that God's strength was more than enough to make up for his own weakness. . .and because he made that leap, we still talk about his triumph today.

FOR FURTHER THOUGHT:

- Why are some men all too willing to point out their weaknesses when God asks them to do something but feel free to brag about their strength to everyone else?

- In what ways has God strengthened you as you've stepped out in faith?

PRAYER STARTER:

God, I know the life of holiness You've laid out before me is more than I can achieve on my own. That's why I'm placing my weakness in Your hands, knowing You'll transform it into strength.

THE SLOW MARCH OF TIME

Do not reject me in the time of old age;
do not forsake me when my strength fails.
PSALM 71:9

Just the act of being human can be terrifying. We can be coasting along just fine when suddenly, as we lie awake in the dead of night, we're struck by a crippling reminder of our own mortality. *What will I do when I'm older,* we may think, *and all my strength is gone?* As we imagine our fingers shriveling and the muscles in our legs wasting away, the sheer helplessness of being unable to stop the slow march of time can be enough to send us into depression.

If you know what it feels like to experience such existential dread, don't worry—the psalmist felt it too. In today's prayer, he pleaded with God to remember him when his hair turned gray and his bones grew feeble. He knew his youthful vigor would one day vanish but that didn't mean he would cease to be strong. He knew God was able to provide a wholly different kind of strength to make it through his silver years—a calmness that would persist until his final breath.

If you're afraid of what the future holds—old age,

sickness, or some other shadowy threat—bring your fear to God and ask Him to fill you with His power. With God by your side, you'll always be a mighty warrior for Christ.

FOR FURTHER THOUGHT:

- Why do you think God allows our bodies to grow old and feeble?

- How would our attitudes toward life and eternity be different if we did not age?

PRAYER STARTER:

Eternal God, I don't like the prospects of growing older, but I know You've taught me to take life one day at a time. I'm confident You'll provide what I need whenever the time comes.

ALL EYES ON HIM

And Jehoshaphat. . .said, "O LORD God of our fathers, are You not God in heaven. . . . who drove out the inhabitants of this land before Your people Israel and gave it to the descendants of Your friend Abraham forever?. . . We have no might against this great company that comes against us, nor do we know what to do. But our eyes are on You."
2 CHRONICLES 20:5–7, 12

At first glance, it appears that Jehoshaphat in today's prayer attempted to remind God of all the things He did, as if God had somehow forgotten. But that's not what happened here. Instead, Jehoshaphat reminded *himself* of God's ability, all while telling God, "I know You can do it again. All eyes are on You."

Have you ever faced an insurmountable challenge, wondering where you could find support? Maybe you or a close family member had fallen deathly ill. Or maybe the pressures of temptations were closing so hotly around you that you didn't know how to resist any longer. No matter your struggle, God is able to take care of it. We know this because we've seen it—in the Bible, in the lives of our Christian friends, and even in our own experiences. Even when our strength is gone and we feel as if we're breathing our last, God can empower us with a second wind.

Today, remind yourself of God's power and embrace the opportunity to share in such strength.

FOR FURTHER THOUGHT:

- How has God shown His power in your life?
- How might reminding yourself of His faithfulness encourage you when the next big problem arises?

PRAYER STARTER:

Holy God, You're more than capable of handling this problem ahead. Give me a small fraction of Your strength so I can face the future with the confidence only You can provide.

WHEN FOOLS BOAST

They all made us afraid, saying, "Their hands shall be weakened from the work so that it is not done." Now, therefore, O God, strengthen my hands.

NEHEMIAH 6:9

Nehemiah had a lot of enemies, and all of them were bent on achieving one goal: to stop Nehemiah from building that wall. "This should be easy," they said, twirling their proverbial mustaches. "We'll just threaten them a little, put some obstacles in their way, and they'll give up in no time. They're nothing but a bunch of weaklings. Ha!"

Unfortunately for them, their plan wasn't exactly a success.

But why wasn't it? Technically, they were right—on their own, the Israelites didn't have a chance of building the wall. It was one guy and a crew of misfits returning from captivity against a host of organized enemies and even a king's decree. Not exactly a fair fight! Surely, it would have been easy to discourage them from such a lofty goal.

But Nehemiah's enemies were forgetting one thing: God had sanctioned the wall's construction, so it *would* be finished. Period. These men weren't working through their own strength; they were being actively strengthened by God Himself. And because of Nehemiah's bold reliance on God, the wall was soon completed, and his enemies were put to shame.

When fools boast of their ability to stand in your way, ask God to strengthen your hands. . .and then keep building.

FOR FURTHER THOUGHT:

- What is the world trying to stop the church from doing today?
- How can knowing God is on your side give you the strength to boldly do it anyway?

PRAYER STARTER:

Father God, strengthen my hands today—and not just my hands but my heart, my soul, and my willpower to work for You. Help me push through and reach this world for You.

CRIPPLING FEAR

Have mercy on me, O Lord, for I am weak.
O Lord, heal me, for my bones are vexed. My soul
is also greatly vexed, but You, O Lord, how long?
PSALM 6:2–3

Today's psalm is a song of desperation—a fervent, frantic plea for strength in the valley of weakness. David's heart had not just been broken but crushed, ground to powder under life's pressure. He felt suffocated in fear, drowning in his own tears (verse 6).

Have you ever been there? Maybe you find yourself nodding in agreement as you read this psalm, sympathizing with David's agonizing plight. You may know all too well what it feels like to have bone-crunching, soul-piercing fear in the dead of night, alone with nowhere to turn. Maybe you're even experiencing such a struggle right now.

If so, cry out to God. You don't have to hide your weakness, afraid He might think of you as less of a man. He already knows. There's nothing you can hold back from His all-seeing eyes. When your soul is vexed, He feels your pain and wants you to run to Him for strength.

Refusing to do so is like drinking poison, thinking it'll make you stronger.

When David cried out for strength, God heard him. . .and He gave him a long and prosperous reign full of His blessings and favor. What's holding you back from doing the same?

FOR FURTHER THOUGHT:

- What do you think would have happened to David had he relied on his own strength?
- How differently would Israel's history have played out?

PRAYER STARTER:

Lord, I'm depending on You to give me strength in this time of weakness. Please take this crippling fear from me and replace it with Your peace.

THE ENDLESS WAR

"And do not lead us into temptation, but deliver us from evil. For Yours is the kingdom and the power and the glory forever. Amen."
MATTHEW 6:13

Maybe you've noticed it by now, but the Christian life isn't as easy as those inspirational songs and smiling preachers on television make it seem. It's tough at times. Gritty. Unruly, like trying to carry a large, jagged stone.

And when it comes to things that make a godly man's life difficult, temptation is perhaps the biggest offender. Opportunities for evil lurk around every corner. Sometimes, a man has to search for them; other times, they're practically smacking him in the face. To push back against such overwhelming darkness, it takes every gram of strength in a man's inventory—and then some.

Jesus knew this more than any man who's ever lived. He faced the devil—the undisputed master of temptation—and came out without a scratch. But there was more. Each day, the growing dread of His crucifixion weighed on His soul. But each day, He successfully fought back the urge to give in. How? By relying on the strength His Father provided.

By acknowledging God as the source of all good things, Jesus—even while in His limited, earthly body—opened Himself up to receiving the infinite strength that His Father possessed. The same is true for each man of God today. No matter how strong you think you are, you aren't strong enough to take on the devil on his home turf. Only God can shield your soul from Satan's endless assaults and give you the strength to endure.

All you have to do is ask.

FOR FURTHER THOUGHT:

- What's the biggest temptation you struggle against?
- When was the last time you implored God to help you defeat it once and for all?

PRAYER STARTER:

Guide me into righteousness, Lord. Teach my soul how to refuse the things my flesh craves.

ALSO FOR GUYS

Guys, you know life can be really hard. But God is bigger than any challenge you face! This 180-entry devotional builds off the inspired truth of 2 Corinthians 12:10, "when I am weak, then I am strong." You'll be encouraged to seek your daily strength from the all-powerful God through Jesus Christ.

Hardback / ISBN 978-1-63609-750-3

Find This and More from Barbour
Publishing at Your Favorite Bookstore
or www.barbourbooks.com